MACARTHUR

★ THE | GENERALS ★

MACARTHUR

Defiant Soldier

★ THE | GENERALS ★

Mitchell Yockelson

THOMAS NELSON
Since 1798

NASHVILLE   DALLAS   MEXICO CITY   RIO DE JANEIRO

Published in Nashville, Tennessee, by Thomas Nelson. Thomas Nelson is a registered trademark of Thomas Nelson, Inc.

Photographs courtesy of the National Archives and Records Administration (NARA) and MacArthur Memorial Archives and Library.

Thomas Nelson, Inc., titles may be purchased in bulk for educational, business, fund-raising, or sales promotional use. For information, please e-mail SpecialMarkets@ThomasNelson.com.

Library of Congress Cataloging-in-Publication Data

ISBN: 9781595552921

Yockelson, Mitchell A., 1962-
   MacArthur : America's general / Mitchell Yockelson.
      p. cm.
   Includes bibliographical references.
   ISBN 978-1-59555-292-1
   1. MacArthur, Douglas, 1880-1964. 2. Generals--United States--Biography. 3. United States. Army--Officers--Biography. 4. United States--History, Military--20th century. I. Title.
   E745.M3Y66 2011
   355.0092--dc22
   [B]

2010048850

Printed in the United States of America

11 12 13 14 15 WOR 6 5 4 3 2 1

Contents

A Note from the Editor

TO CONTEMPLATE THE lives of America's generals is to behold both the best of us as a nation and the lesser angels of human nature, to bask in genius and to be repulsed by arrogance and folly. It is these dichotomies that have defined the widely differing attitudes toward the "man on horseback," which have alternatively shaped the eras of our national memory. We have had our seasons of hagiography, in which our commanders can do no wrong and in which they are presented to the young, in particular, as unerring examples of nobility and manhood. We have had our revisionist seasons, in which all power corrupts—military power in particular—and in which the general is a reviled symbol of societal ills.

Fortunately, we have matured. We have left our adolescence

with its gushing extremes and have come to a more temperate view. Now, we are capable as a nation of celebrating Washington's gifts to us while admitting that he was not always a gifted tactician in the field. We can honor Patton's battlefield genius and decry the deformities of soul which diminished him. We can learn both from MacArthur at Inchon and from MacArthur at Wake Island.

We can also move beyond the mythologies of film and leaden textbook to know the vital humanity and the agonizing conflicts, to find a literary experience of war which puts the smell of boot leather and canvas in the nostrils and both the horror and the glory of battle in the heart. This will endear our nation's generals to us and help us learn the lessons they have to teach. Of this we are in desperate need, for they offer lessons of manhood in an age of androgyny, of courage in an age of terror, of prescience in an age of myopia, and of self-mastery in an age of sloth. To know their story and their meaning, then, is the goal here and in the hope that we will emerge from the experience a more learned, perhaps more gallant, and, certainly, more grateful people.

Stephen Mansfield
Series Editor, *The Generals*

Introduction

NOT SINCE ULYSSES S. Grant had a military figure so captivated a nation, and Grant was likely adored by only half of the United States. The entire country loved MacArthur.

When he addressed Congress in 1951 in his "Old Soldiers Never Die" speech, he was the most popular man in America. During a military career that spanned fifty-two years and included service in three major wars, MacArthur admirers included an adoring public as well as the soldiers who proudly served under his command on the battlefields of the Western Front, the Pacific Theater, and Korea.

Living in the shadow of his famous father, Arthur MacArthur, Douglas had set forth early to achieve greatness as a gentleman, a scholar, and a hero. These aspirations were fulfilled, and earned him more than one hundred military decorations, including the Medal of Honor. During World War II, at the peak of his popularity, MacArthur captivated the hearts and minds of the American people, who hung on his every word and clamored for news about his actions in the Pacific. He relished every bit of this attention and manipulated the press as he saw fit. Still, his accomplishments in the Philippines and Japan were unrivaled. MacArthur set the bar as a soldier-statesman and in tribute there are schools, roads, bridges, parks, and nearly every other kind of public structure named for Douglas MacArthur the world over.

His life was not without flaws, however, as revealed by controversies such as MacArthur's response to the Bonus Marchers in 1932 and his outspoken criticism of President Truman that lead to his dismissal from the army he so dearly loved. Contradictions, exaggerations, and controversy filled his life, as they have the lives of many great leaders. Most who were acquainted with him either loved or hated him. One biographer, William Manchester, incorrectly deemed him an "American Caesar." This implies that MacArthur was a conqueror and a ruler. Neither is true, although MacArthur's brilliant strategy in the Pacific during World War II, which led to the liberation of the Philippines, was certainly a conquering of the Japanese force. "American Caesar" also implies that he had political aspirations, which he did. His true love, though, was the army and MacArthur felt most comfortable in its embrace. Americans have always clamored for heroes. Before modern television and movies, military commanders had been America's most beloved heroes and MacArthur was among the last of this genre, flaws and all.

MacArthur's faith was also of the utmost importance to him. Although he rarely visited a house of worship, his speeches and messages often referenced God and it is said that he read the Bible every day. His men knew that he looked to God for guidance in the field and this was critical to his command presence in a day in which public faith was still honored.

MacArthur was, in spiritual as in most other matters, ever a nonconformist. From the way he wore his uniform to his command style, he stood out among his peers. This helped to make him an icon and inspired Hollywood to try to capture him in several films. Gregory Peck gave a sympathetic portrayal of him in the 1976 big screen production *MacArthur*. Peck and the film's producers went to great lengths to achieve historic accuracy. The "Duty, Honor, Country" speech which encases the movies was filmed at West Point in front of two regiments of cadets. The movie follows MacArthur from the commencement of World War I through the relief of his command by President Truman in 1951 and does so with compassion and attention to detail. It was well received at the box office. The same cannot be said for the movie *Inchon*, in which Laurence Olivier played the role of MacArthur. Audiences rejected the film, mostly because Unification Church founder Sun Myung Moon financed its production. It cost almost forty-six million dollars to make and took in only two million dollars at the box office after it was released in the United States and Canada in May 1981.

Television also poked fun at MacArthur in one episode of the enormously popular series *M*A*S*H*, set during the Korean War. When the episode depicting MacArthur was broadcast in

1982, it was the first introduction many young Americans had to the figure an earlier generation had venerated. M*A*S*H portrayed the popular image of MacArthur with his trademark field-marshal cap, sunglasses, and a corncob pipe proudly displayed.

Who was the real Douglas MacArthur? Historians will argue this question for centuries to come, but we cannot solve the matter definitively here. What we can do is offer fitting tribute and honor the heroic general by lovingly introducing him to a new generation, a generation that knows only the caricature and the myth. In this way we can hope that his character and his sense of duty will be embedded in a people among whom he has tragically dimmed in memory.

ONE

The MacArthurs

DOUGLAS MACARTHUR IDOLIZED his father, Lieutenant General Arthur MacArthur, and for good reason. The elder MacArthur was intelligent, possessed high professional standards, and—most appealing to an impressionable young man with military ambitions of his own—General Arthur MacArthur was fearless in combat. Although largely forgotten today and certainly overshadowed by his famous son, the senior MacArthur was one of America's greatest soldiers. Douglas believed that he could never equal his father, but he looked to him as a role model. And throughout his own career Douglas certainly emulated his father, for better and for worse.

Tracing the MacArthur lineage is complicated and some of the facts passed down through the years are questionable. Arthur's father, also named Arthur, and later known as Judge MacArthur, was the patriarch of the family. He was born on January 26, 1817, in Glasgow, Scotland. Coincidentally, his mother's surname was also MacArthur. As the story goes, the earliest MacArthurs descended from Highlander nobility and a rich Scottish military heritage that dated to the sixth century.

Arthur Jr. never knew his father or his sister. They both died just days before he was born, and relatives looked after mother and son. His mother, Sarah, remarried in 1824 and a few years later the family immigrated to the United States to join one of Sarah's sisters in Uxbridge, Massachusetts, a booming textile town about sixty miles south of Boston.[1] Arthur attended the one-room Uxbridge Academy until an economic downturn forced it to close and he transferred to a boarding school in Amherst, Massachusetts. He then enrolled briefly at Wesleyan College in Middletown, Connecticut, before moving to New York City to clerk in a law firm. Along the way he married Aurelia, the daughter of a wealthy Chicopee, Massachusetts, industrialist, and supported his wife by opening his own law office in Springfield, Massachusetts. On June 2, 1845, the young couple had a son, who was named for his father. Four years later the family moved to Milwaukee, Wisconsin, where Arthur Sr. continued to practice law, but also dabbled in politics. Some years later he served as lieutenant governor and for five days as governor of the state. Ever the public servant, Arthur Sr. was elected circuit court judge for two terms and earned the moniker "Judge MacArthur."[2]

When the Civil War commenced, Arthur Jr. was eager to join in support of the Union. Throughout his young life he had devoured books on military and historical subjects and now came the opportunity to make history himself. Judge MacArthur felt his son was not ready for the army, though, and sent him to a private military school for a year. In 1862 he attempted to secure a presidential appointment for Arthur Jr. at West Point. The judge wrote the U.S. senator from Wisconsin and through him father and son visited President Abraham Lincoln at the White House. Lincoln told them the bad news that there were no more presidential vacancies until the next year. Arthur Jr. refused to wait and enlisted in the 24th Wisconsin Infantry Regiment.

Through his father's influence he gained a commission as first lieutenant and was assigned the position of regimental adjutant. Not content to be just a clerk, Arthur Jr. saw his first action in October 1862, when the regiment supported a division in the Army of the Ohio near Perryville, Kentucky. Young MacArthur gave a good account of himself and the division commander, Brigadier General Philip A. Sheridan, cited Arthur Jr. for gallantry under fire and promoted him to brevet captain. At the end of 1862, the 24th Wisconsin took part in the heavy fighting at Stones River, Tennessee, and Captain MacArthur was again praised for his gallantry while under fire.

Now a combat veteran, his finest moment on the battlefield occurred during the Battle of Missionary Ridge near Chattanooga, Tennessee, on November 25, 1863. There, the 24th Wisconsin, with other Union regiments, captured Confederate-held rifle pits on the ridge. Not willing to rest on their laurels, the regiment took the initiative and charged up the steep, rocky face of the ridge to route Confederates entrenched at the crest. During the action the 24th's color bearer was hit. MacArthur, seeing the wounded soldier about to fall, grabbed the regimental flag from him and planted it on the crest of the ridge, thus proving the Wisconsin troops had reached the top first.

Impressed by the act of bravery, the regimental commander, Major Carl von Baumach, wrote in his official report that MacArthur "was the most distinguished in action on a field where many in the regiment displayed conspicuous gallantry, worthy of the highest praise."[3] Much later MacArthur received the Medal of Honor for his showing that day. When Douglas received the same coveted decoration during World War II, they were the first father and son in American history to have earned such distinction.

Two months after Missionary Ridge, Arthur was promoted to major and placed in command of the 24th Wisconsin. He led the regiment as it took part in General William T. Sherman's Atlanta campaign and was wounded while attacking a heavily entrenched enemy position at Kennesaw Mountain. It took almost two months for his wounds to heal, and when he returned to the battlefield on November 30, 1864, he was wounded again during the battle at Franklin, Tennessee. This time he was shot in the leg and through the breast, and the war now ended for him. MacArthur was again cited for gallantry and, as a result, promoted to brevet colonel and eventually to the permanent rank of lieutenant colonel of volunteers. He always insisted on leading his men at the front, a heroic trait his son adopted during World War I.

Arthur Jr. mustered out of the service in June 1865 and returned to Milwaukee unsure of his future. He studied law under his father's guidance for several months but missed the army and the glory it brought him. Given the state of the post–Civil War regular army with its downsizing, rejoining the military was not looked upon favorably as a career choice. But MacArthur was sure this was what he wanted, so he sought endorsements from generals and senators and was commissioned as second lieutenant. Shortly thereafter he was made a captain.

Army service after the Civil War meant either reconstruction duty in the South or fighting Indians in the West. Arthur experienced both. Captain MacArthur was ordered to serve with the 36th Infantry Regiment. Posted at Fort Kearney in Nebraska Territory, the regiment was charged with protecting emigrants traversing the Oregon Trail and workers constructing the Union Pacific Railroad. As the railroad crews accomplished their work and headed west through Nebraska, Colorado, and Wyoming, they were protected by the ten companies that comprised the 36th Infantry.

Before long the regiment moved to Fort Sanders, Colorado, where they performed a dual role as a police force and labor brigade. With the construction of the railroad came mining camps, cow towns, and farming communities. The residents of each needed protection. They were easy prey for marauding Indians who felt infringed upon by the new settlers and the bands of outlaws. The 36th was expected to keep law and order, as well as build bridges, telegraph lines, and roads. Somehow they also found time for military drill and guard duty.

After two years at Sanders, the 36th was sent to Fort Bridger, Wyoming, also to protect the Union Pacific and the settlers and crews who followed the railroad. Then a year later the regimental officers learned that Congress was reducing the army from forty to twenty-five regiments and the 36th was one of the units to be abolished. Captain McArthur was now without a job. He went back to Milwaukee in May 1869 to wait things out. Reality sunk in that perhaps the military, was too unstable and that maybe he should reconsider a law career, as his father had wanted.

Arthur had never completely given up the idea of becoming an attorney and had brought his law books with him when he joined the 36th. Just three months after returning home he took the Wisconsin bar examinations and passed them. But the army called again and he never had the chance to put his law degree into practice. The War Department ordered him to New York City for assignment at the Cavalry Recruiting Office in the Bowery.

Keeping officers in the army was never a problem, but retaining enlisted men was, as exhibited by the high desertion rate. New York was an ideal place for recruitment since there was always a steady stream of immigrants right off the boat needing employment. Then there was the ready supply of ruffians in the poorer sections of the city who were always looking for action and could easily be convinced to join the army and fight Indians. MacArthur took on his new assignment with vigor, studying cavalry tactics to make his pitch as a recruiting officer more believable. And the more he learned about the cavalry, the more he felt he wanted to serve in this branch.

Ironically General Philip Sheridan, now a commander of the Division of the Missouri, came to New York and he and MacArthur became reacquainted. Sheridan liked MacArthur's enthusiasm and endorsed him as a cavalry officer. For unknown reasons, the War Department ignored Sheridan's recommendation and instead assigned MacArthur to the 13th Infantry Regiment when his current post was up. This sent him back to the West for the same duty as before, guarding the construction of railroad lines.

After moving from one post to another, the 36th Infantry was consolidated with the 7th Infantry Regiment. Even though the U.S. Army was actively campaigning against the Indians, Arthur saw none of this. Eight years in the army had earned him not a single campaign badge. Eventually he transferred to the 13th Infantry and remained in the West until the regiment was reassigned to Jackson Barracks, Louisiana, in 1874. The city was located about fifty miles north of New Orleans and on the west bank of the Mississippi River. The regiment was assigned the difficult task of protecting the presidentially appointed reconstruction governor, William P. Kellogg. His administration was widely known to be corrupt, and the Republication governor of Louisiana and the occupying army were seen as an extension of Washington's problems.[4]

As MacArthur approached the third decade of his life he was eager to settle down and have a family. Service on the frontier afforded little opportunity to meet a young lady for marriage, but nearby New Orleans provided the opportunity. There he attended balls and dances and his chance to find a wife drastically improved. A Mardi Gras celebration proved to be his lucky moment, and there he met a Southern belle named Mary Pinkney Hardy. Called Pinky by her family and friends, she stole Arthur's heart and they fell deeply in love.

Pinky was born in 1852 at Riveredge, her family's plantation near Norfolk. The Hardy family had a long military tradition, serving under George Washington's command during the American Revolution and continuing with four brothers who fought in the Confederacy. Pinky was of Scottish descent, and with the family's military background, MacArthur was certain he had found his match. She was also quite pretty and a graduate of the Mount de Sales Academy girls school where young women learned to dance, embroider, paint, and generally master the skills that were important to ladies of that era. Later on, as a wife and mother, Pinky became a "complex woman, being both meek and tough, petulant and sentimental, charming and emotional," according to biographer William Manchester. "Under her mannered, pretty exterior, she was cool, practical, and absolutely determined."[5]

When Union Army forces under General Benjamin Butler occupied Norfolk, they had made the Hardy estate a headquarters. The family fled to their summer home in Henderson, North Carolina, and remained there until the war ended and it was safe to go back to Riveredge. At first Pinky's family frowned upon her decision to marry a Yankee. After all, the Civil War had only recently ended and the Hardys were proud Southerners. Winning them over required a visit to Riveredge by Judge MacArthur, who used his charm and Scottish humor to ease the family's animosities and secure a bride for his son. Despite Judge's efforts, though, two of Pinky's diehard Confederate brothers refused to accept their new brother-in-law and stayed away from the May 1875 wedding.[6]

Pinky had no idea what to expect when marrying an army officer. Luckily, her husband's next assignment was in Washington and thus spared Pinky, for the time being, from life on a frontier post. She was going to live in a big city and become exposed to the culture that came with the experience. The year she and her husband spent in Washington is described by Arthur's biographer as one of the happiest times of their marriage.[7] While he mainly served on examining and retirement boards, Pinky indulged the company of Judge MacArthur and the Washington elite he knew well. The newlyweds were invited to meet and attend parties with congressmen, senators, and prominent businessmen. Pinky enjoyed this socializing much more than her husband did. In his eyes some of the political elite were corrupt and he kept as far away from them as possible. It was also a joyous time for the MacArthurs. Pinky returned to Norfolk and gave birth to their first son, named Arthur III.

At the end of 1876, Arthur Jr. was sent back to Louisiana to again serve with the 13th Regiment at Jackson Barracks. He was placed in command of Company K. Life there was a far cry from what they had just experienced in Washington. The post dated from 1831 and because Congress appropriated little money for maintaining the infrastructure of military installations, many of its buildings were in disrepair. The MacArthurs were quartered in a cramped officer's cottage.

Pinky learned to adapt to the routine of army life but used Louisiana's dreadfully hot summers as an excuse to travel back to Riveredge to be with her family. There was even more reason to return home in the summer of 1878—she was pregnant with their second child and expected to deliver that autumn. Jefferson Barracks did not have the family support found in Riveredge, so

Pinky remained in the east when the MacArthurs' second son, Malcolm, was born.

Meanwhile Captain MacArthur spent much of his time drilling and inspecting his men, coupled with the occasional detached duty that involved breaking up labor disputes. He was every bit the family man and rarely fraternized with other officers. He preferred a quiet army life and was seldom seen at the officers club or at social affairs. MacArthur's main interest was his sons. The eldest, Arthur III, accompanied his father's troops on short supply excursions.

With occupation duty coming to an end in the South, regiments were shifted to various army posts. Company K moved frequently throughout Louisiana and Arkansas. In 1880, the last year Arthur MacArthur served in the region, Pinky was pregnant again. Her intention, as she had done with Arthur III and Malcolm, was to deliver at Riveredge. The child, whom the MacArthurs named Douglas, had other ideas and arrived sooner than expected on January 26, 1880. That same day Judge MacArthur turned sixty-three. The infant, who later eclipsed the greatness of his father and grandfather, was born at Little Rock Arsenal. Even though he entered the world far from Norfolk, the city still took pride in Douglas's arrival and he never forgot this. Norfolk's newspapers covered the event with headlines that oddly read: "Douglas MacArthur was born on January 26, while his parents were away."[8]

Education of a Soldier

AFTER DOUGLAS WAS born, Captain MacArthur moved
with his family to the next assignment at Fort Wingate, New
Mexico. A remote post about one hundred miles northwest of
Albuquerque, it served as a garrison for the 13th Infantry and a
couple of cavalry companies. The soldiers guarded crews building
the Atchison, Topeka and Santa Fe Railroad, while the mounted
troops chased after Apache Indians. Pinky absolutely hated Fort
Wingate. There were few other women for her to socialize with
and the living conditions were abysmal. The MacArthurs were
quartered in an adobe structure with two rooms and a kitchen—
far too small for a family of five. Only a front porch provided some
comfort during the brutally hot New Mexico summers.

Pinky continually urged her husband to resign his commission to practice law or to go into business. Arthur refused. He was comfortable with army life and willing to accept its difficulties in hopes that his patience would lead to a promotion and a better assignment. In later years, Douglas MacArthur would often recall Wingate with fondness.

> Life at Fort Wingate was packed with adventure. Stories and rumors of notorious outlaws circulated often in the little world within the walls of the fort. Indians, whether sullen Chiricahua prisoners or peaceful Navaho sheepherders were a daily sight . . . For young and old at Wingate, the highlight of the year was the Fourth of July when parades, shooting contests, sack races, and other competitions marked the joyous celebration from early morning until late in the evening.[1]

Even more, the experience instilled in young Douglas the thrill of wearing a uniform and serving one's country. He often said, "My first recollection is that of a bugle call." Each morning he rose early and joined the soldiers of the 13th Infantry Regiment as they stood at rigid attention. Proudly he watched as his father called muster. It was a "never ending thrill," Douglas later remembered.

Much to Pinky's delight her husband was granted an extended leave from Wingate in April 1882 and the MacArthurs headed to Riveredge to be with her family. Captain MacArthur took advantage of the close proximity to Washington and visited with his father. A month later he was sent back to New Mexico, while Pinky and the children remained in Norfolk. After several months by himself, MacArthur was granted another leave and reunited with his wife and sons in Virginia.

During the spring of 1883, all three children were struck with measles. Tragically, Malcolm died at age four. The MacArthurs were devastated and grief stricken. Pinky believed Douglas and Arthur III had survived for a reason and that they should seize the opportunity by distinguishing themselves in life. She specifically told Douglas, "You must grow up to be a great man—like your father and Robert E. Lee." Because he was the youngest child, Pinky was especially drawn to Douglas and their relationship remained strong until her death some fifty years later. Douglas took the loss extremely hard since Malcolm was closest to him in age and had been his playmate.[2]

In June 1883 the MacArthurs moved back to Fort Wingate. Because of Malcolm's death it was not a happy time for the family. Arthur avoided social contact with other officers and became more isolated than usual. Pinky once again encouraged him to resign his commission and return to civilian life, but Arthur was accustomed to the army and believed there were better times ahead if he would just remain patient. Such opportunity came several months later when Captain MacArthur was given an independent command at a small post three hundred miles south of Fort Wingate near the Rio Grande River, called Fort Selden. Despite the rough conditions of the fort, with its crude, run-down buildings, it was an ideal setting for the MacArthurs at this time. For Arthur it meant little interference from superior officers and that he could operate the fort as he pleased. Pinky also liked the assignment at Selden—its remoteness and the absence of other officers relinquished her of social obligation. As Arthur's biographer points out, the two and a half years at Fort Selden helped the family "heal from the wounds caused by Malcolm's death."[3]

Three years later Captain MacArthur's perseverance paid off. Company K was detached and sent to the Infantry and Cavalry School at Fort Leavenworth, Kansas. It was a welcome change for the family. They were provided a nice apartment and Pinky frequented the nearby stores, theaters, and restaurants with other officers' wives. Douglas and his brother enrolled in the post school and both impressed their teachers as great students. For the first time Pinky enjoyed her association with the army. She was even happier during the summer of 1889 when her husband was promoted to major and named assistant adjutant general. Judge MacArthur had a hand in the new assignment, but it didn't matter how it happened, the MacArthurs were returning to Washington.

Even though Douglas missed the excitement of frontier life, he now had the wonderful opportunity to spend time with his grandfather, who mingled with the Washington elite. The grandeur rubbed off on Douglas. He later called it "my first glimpse of politics and diplomacy, statesmanship and intrigue." Judge MacArthur's frequent discussions with his grandson instilled in Douglas the idea that a military career was more than just wearing a uniform and barking out orders. "You must also be a gentleman and scholar and above all else, honorable." This meant no lying or cheating.

The judge "was noted for his dry wit," Douglas recalled, "and I could listen to anecdotes for hours." His grandfather also taught him to play poker. During the last hand they played together,

Douglas was certain he had him beat. "I held four queens and in my elation bet every chip I had," he remembered. Judge Arthur then laid down four kings, shocking his grandson. He told him, "Dear boy, nothing is sure in this life. Everything is relative."[4]

Major MacArthur was also glad to be back in Washington. Not only was it a pleasure to be with his father again, he was fulfilled professionally as well. His primary task was redrafting regulations that laid the foundation for reform of the army in later years, and this afforded him the chance to dip into his legal background.

There was another reason he enjoyed being at the War Department. Twenty-six years after he heroically led the 24th Wisconsin during the Battle of Missionary Ridge, Arthur MacArthur finally received the Medal of Honor. He had learned that another officer, First Lieutenant Matthias W. Day, was being considered for the medal because of bravery during the Apache war. Arthur Jr. had always thought the nation's highest military honor was only awarded to enlisted men and never questioned why his application had been rejected. After Day's was approved, Major MacArthur put in for his and the review board agreed. Douglas and his brother were elated about their father's accomplishment, and although Arthur Jr. rarely spoke of his heroic deeds, Judge MacArthur often told of his son's Civil War service, even at the risk of embellishment.

Sadly, Judge MacArthur only lived until 1896, and during the last five years of his life he was mostly in ill health with the "grippe," the former name for influenza. His death at eighty-one was a sad time for the MacArthurs, although Douglas, who was sixteen at the time, made no mention of the passing in his memoirs. His grandfather's legacy and the many prominent friends he left behind benefited Douglas a couple of years later when he applied to West Point. Major MacArthur was no longer in Washington when the family patriarch died. The MacArthurs had moved a few years before to San Antonio, Texas, so Arthur Jr. could take over as assistant general for the Department of Texas.

Douglas's older brother was out of the family home by then, having accepted an appointment to the Naval Academy. Continuing the family's martial tradition, Douglas entered the West Texas Military Academy in San Antonio as one of its first students when the school opened in 1893. Founded by Episcopal bishop Reverend James S. Johnston, the academy was a perfect setting for Douglas. At fourteen, he needed an academic challenge and the academy gave him just that. Situated on Government Hill overlooking the Alamo and the city of San Antonio, Douglas excelled and developed a "desire to know." His father played an active role in his life then, often attending the academy's baseball and football games, as well as watching his son play tennis.

Douglas developed a deep spiritual interest while in San Antonio. He attended his new school equipped with a Bible, the Book of Common Prayer, and a hymnbook.[5] On April 1, 1894, MacArthur was confirmed at St. Paul's Memorial Church, in the same chapel where the academy cadets assembled each day for services. From this point forward he read the Bible daily and although he did not attend church on a regular basis, almost always his speeches referenced the Almighty. He said the "biblical lessons began to open the spiritual portals of a growing faith."[6]

Douglas excelled academically at West Texas Academy, winning medals in Latin, mathematics, and competitive speaking. He also proved a natural athlete and during his senior year he quarterbacked the undefeated football team in the fall and played shortstop on the baseball team in the spring. Besides such activities he found time to join the school's elite cadet drill team appropriately named the Crack Squad. Much to the delight of his parents, in June 1897 Douglas MacArthur graduated valedictorian with a four-year grade point average of 97.33. Intellectually he had risen to the expectations of his grandfather and father.

Next, Douglas set his sights on the United States Military Academy. One of his grandfather's old friends, Congressman Theobald Ojten, offered to appoint Douglas to West Point under two conditions. First, he had to live in the congressman's Milwaukee district; and second, he had to outscore other applicants in competitive exams. Neither proved to be a problem. In October 1897, Colonel MacArthur was assigned as the Department of Dakota adjutant general and while its headquarters were in St. Paul, Minnesota, he moved his wife and son to the Plankinton House in Milwaukee, 330 miles away. Douglas enrolled in the local high school and also received private tutoring. As always, his father made sure he was directly involved in his son's life, so he took the train home on the weekends to be with him and Pinky.

The high school was a two-mile walk from the hotel where Douglas and his mother stayed. Between classes during the day and tutoring afterward, MacArthur later said, "I never worked harder in my life." When the important day in early June 1898 finally arrived, he was petrified. "The night before the examinations," MacArthur said, "for the first time in my life I could not sleep, and the next morning when I arrived at the city hall I felt nauseated."

But Pinky gave him a pep talk and her words of wisdom pulled Douglas through this tough ordeal. "Doug, she said, you'll win if you don't lose your nerve. You must believe in yourself, my son, or no one else will believe in you. Be self-confident, self-reliant, and even if you don't make it, you will know you have done your best. Now, go to it."[7] And that he did.

When the exams were graded, MacArthur came out on top. The local newspaper covered the examination as if it had been a political election. "He Will Go to West Point," the June 7, 1898, *Milwaukee Journal* reported. The headline was followed by a detailed account of how "young MacArthur" bested his opponents by a wide margin because of his "determination to win after studying very hard." In all likelihood a proud Pinky helped the reporter craft his story. Douglas later said, "Careful preparation had repaid me. It was a lesson I never forgot. Preparedness is the key to success and victory."[8]

Two months prior to the exam, the United States declared war on Spain after the USS *Maine* blew up in the Havana, Cuba, harbor on February 15, 1898, killing 212 Americans. Yellow journalists assured the public and President William McKinley that the explosion was not an accident but an act of sabotage by the Spanish. McKinley bought into this and America embarked on what was later called "a splendid little war." Major MacArthur was now a brigadier general of volunteers in the Philippines, where he led an infantry brigade during the Battle of Manila.

Arthur III served in the other theater of war aboard the *Vixen*, and took part in the Battle of Santiago, Cuba. While his father and brother were off to war, Douglas had to wait another year before entering West Point. According to William Manchester, it would take that long to cure his spinal curvature problem and pass the physical exam.[9]

Wearing a light-colored fedora, Douglas disembarked from a West Shore Railroad train on June 13, 1899, and got his first glance at West Point. Joining him on that warm Tuesday afternoon was Pinky. She was not there to see her son off to college and then return home. With her husband in the Philippines, Pinky had nowhere else to go and would remain at West Point for the entire four years her son was a cadet. As awkward as that sounds, it seemed appropriate to have her by his side while at the military academy.

During his formative years, influential men such as his father and grandfather had surrounded Douglas, and they no doubt shaped his outlook on life, but Pinky, in many respects, had the greatest impact on him. She always knew the correct things to say at the appropriate moment. "Do what is right, no matter what the personal sacrifice might be. Our country is always to come first," Pinky once told her youngest son. "Two things we must never do: lie or tattle."[10] At West Point Douglas often turned to his mother for advice. They usually met up for a short period just before the evening meal.

Douglas commenced summer camp, while his mother checked into her new residence at Craney's Hotel, an antebellum structure that stood on the northern edge of West Point Plain. It was constructed of yellow brick and had a broad green wooden veranda that at one time must have been impressive, but by the summer of 1899 the hotel was showing its age. Eventually it was torn down and the site became a parking lot.[11] Supposedly Pinky had a bird's-eye view into barracks Room 1123 and she could observe by the lamplight whether her son was studying.[12]

Summer camp took place during the two months prior to the commencement of classes and was notorious for the brutal hazing directed at plebes. MacArthur's experience was especially tough for a number of reasons. Pinky's presence a short distance from his dorm labeled MacArthur a "mother's boy," but even worse, his father was a famous general frequently in the news because of the situation in the Philippines. This made the general's son the focus of harsh attention from fellow cadets. Luckily for MacArthur, one of his plebe classmates that summer was Ulysses S. Grant III, the grandson of the famous general and president. Grant's mother also took up residence at Craney's. That and his pedigree made him a target of harassment, but nowhere on the same level as MacArthur. Nonetheless, MacArthur at least had someone he could commiserate with and perhaps absorb some of the abuse that otherwise would have been directed his way.

Much of MacArthur's hazing was undertaken strictly for laughs, such as forcing him to make funny speeches or recite his father's military record. Another time he was required to stay immobile for an hour. This was all part of "Beast Barracks," when a plebe spent his first three weeks at West Point living in a tent while subjected to all forms of harassment. Failure to participate in the activities resulted in severe punishment by an upper classman. There were several other incidents that tested MacArthur both mentally and physically and these were no joke.

For instance, he was ordered to perform 250 challenging "spread eagles" and 200 "wooden willies" one night in a darkened tent. The first exercise required MacArthur to squat and rise over broken glass while at the same time flapping his arms like wings. A wooden willy was even more tiresome. This involved taking his rifle and drawing it up to the position of fire, then dropping it to the position of ready. His tormenters expected him to fail miserably while performing both tasks, but MacArthur was not willing to give them such satisfaction. He arrived at West Point in great shape and with his honed athletic ability MacArthur performed 200 of the difficult exercises before passing out from fatigue.

When he awoke MacArthur suffered from severe arm and leg spasms. To further test his dignity a short time later, he was given a sweat bath where he was forced to dress in full uniform, wear a raincoat, then wrap blankets over his clothes while staying all night in a small tent in the summer heat. Much like his entrance exam, he passed this test with flying colors.[13]

MacArthur survived Beast Barracks well beyond expectations and earned the approval of the upperclassmen for his poise and courage. It was clear from the onset that he was going to be a leader of men. One of his classmates, Robert E. Wood, was not only impressed with MacArthur's fortitude under stress, but with his physical presence as well. Wood thought that he was "without a doubt the handsomest cadet that ever came into the academy, six-foot tall, and slender with a fine body and dark flashing eyes." Another classmate described MacArthur as "brilliant, absolutely fearless." While yet another recalled him as "a typical westerner" with "a ruddy, outdoors complexion." But as William Manchester pointed out, all these memories of MacArthur were written many years after the writers had encountered him. In reality he entered West Point at five feet eleven inches tall and weighed 133 pounds.[14]

While a cadet, MacArthur was required to testify on three occasions about the practice of hazing. His first testimony was before a board of inquiry called by the superintendent to investigate that summer's hazing, which was deemed harsher than usual. Although privately condoned, as a rule it was forbidden and the penalty was dismissal. MacArthur was among the cadets required to talk about his own hazing and more damaging, name the upper classmen who had hazed him. This put him in an awkward position since implicating a fellow cadet would break the code of honor, but keeping quiet would probably mean expulsion. As in the terrifying experience of his entrance exam, MacArthur became nauseous at the thought of the task that confronted him.

Pinky, close at hand, offered her son the comfort he needed during this strenuous ordeal: "Remember the world will be quick in its blame if shadow or shame ever darken your name. Like mother like son, is saying so true, the world will judge mother by you." Then in a postscript she reminded him: "Never lie, never tattle."[15]

MacArthur, in a brilliant move, figured out a way to satisfy everyone. He went before the board of inquiry and named cadets who had already confessed or were already expelled. He mentioned no other names. The next year a cadet died from severe hazing and a military court of inquiry was convened, followed by a special committee of the House of Representatives. In both instances MacArthur remained cool under pressure during his testimonies. Despite the grilling he received, MacArthur again only implicated former cadets and those already confessing their guilt. He held up well, despite becoming nauseous during one of the testimonies. The whole experience proved invaluable since he would go before Congress countless times in the not-so-distant future.

Besides serving as her son's chief adviser, Pinky also helped Douglas and some of his cadet friends enjoy some semblance of a social life. They had little free time and were not allowed leave to go home at Thanksgiving, Christmas, or Easter. Cadets could only step beyond the gates for special reasons, such as parental visits to Craney's.

The academy sponsored various events, however, and on one occasion MacArthur and several other cadets planned to attend a dance. Their dates arrived the evening before and the excited young men were anxious to meet their lady friends. To do so would require Pinky's help. It didn't take much effort on her part since the girls were staying at Craney's. At an appointed time MacArthur and his friends snuck out to the hotel and met their dates in a hallway. While the couples chatted, Mrs. MacArthur kept watch for officers arriving at the hotel to use the telephone. Sure enough, after a short while, one was spotted entering the door of Craney's. In an instant Pinky whisked the cadets downstairs to hide out until she gave the all clear.

Pinky, in fact, provided lookout for Douglas and his friends many other times and she went from being a source of some ridicule to a beloved friend of the lonely cadets. Nevertheless, it is hard to say how MacArthur really felt about having his mother nearby. His West Point chapter in *Reminiscences* mentions her only once.

With or without his mother's help, MacArthur was no different than most young men and liked to take risks when the opportunity presented itself. As he put it, "I worked hard and I played hard." In *Reminiscences* MacArthur tells of a time that a tactical officer saw him publicly kissing a girl on Flirtation Walk. Instead of reporting him for "unbecoming conduct," the officer "just grinned and said 'Congratulations, Mr. MacArthur.'" A more brazen situation occurred during his third year when the cadets were allowed to attend a horse show in New York. Although heavily chaperoned, MacArthur and two others slipped away to Rector's, an infamous bar on Broadway. There they "shook hands with Diamond Jim Brady" and between the three downed nine martinis, much to the astonishment of the bartender. Then MacArthur and his pals "swanked out to a burlesque show." MacArthur's summation? "We loved it." [16]

Such outlandish behavior was of no surprise to anyone who knew MacArthur in those days. As a West Point cadet he commenced to display signs as a non-conformist, a trait that delighted some, while infuriating others who observed him as future commander. He was far more dashing and ambitious then most men his age. The way MacArthur wore his uniform, the confidence he exuded and the desire to question authority made him stand out among others. He did not always play by the rules. Some of this was certainly theater, MacArthur wanting attention. But in most instances when he confronted superiors MacArthur did so because of a belief that he better knew them and backing down showed weakness. His parents encouraged him to be self-assured and he followed their advice with little concern for potential consequences. West Point has graduated many great leaders, before and after MacArthur, but none left their mark on the institution as he had.

Major General Arthur MacArthur in the Philippines.

Mrs. Mary Pinckney "Pinky" MacArthur.

West Point class photograph of MacArthur (1903).

THREE

Douglas Comes of Age

IN THE CLASSROOM, Douglas MacArthur contin-
ued where he had left off at the West Texas Military Academy.
His marks at West Point were impressive, especially given the
restricted educational environment offered there. No matter the
field of study, the teaching method was the same. Cadets were
taught to learn primarily by memorization, which meant reciting
each day's assignment either orally or by writing it on the black-
board. Professors rarely lectured, or for that matter, explained
the topic to any great extent. They were simply there to grade
a cadet's performance. Such an archaic system of teaching frus-
trated MacArthur; he had been wonderfully spoiled by the
stimulating conversations he had with his grandfather as a youth.
Obviously, MacArthur adapted well, graduating first in his class

despite having little time to study. Sports and his nomination as captain of the corps of cadets his last year became his chief priorities and devoured his time.

During one unforgettable moment in the classroom, MacArthur was called upon to recite Einstein's complex space and time relationship, which eventually became the famous theory of relativity. MacArthur nervously stood before the class recalling word for word what he had memorized from the assigned reading. Then to his horror, the professor asked if he understood what it meant. "No sir," he responded, and then surprisingly the instructor replied, "Neither do I, Mister MacArthur. Section dismissed."

In another instance, this time in math class, MacArthur challenged his professor's insistence that he take the final exam. Since he had the highest math average at West Point, the headstrong cadet believed he should be exempt from the final, which was then a standard practice. The instructor, Lieutenant Colonel Wright P. Edgerton, said MacArthur had missed several quizzes due to illness and was expected to report on final examination day. Undeterred, MacArthur offered to resign, rather than take the exam. The professor backed down and MacArthur got his way. This was the first of many times the future general used his powers of persuasion to win an argument.

Outside of the classroom, athletics remained important. MacArthur believed physical fitness was an essential part of being a cadet and that even if someone had no skill, sports should be enjoyed anyway. MacArthur chose to play baseball and on the diamond he was a dependable fielder, a good runner, but a below-average hitter. Much to his delight he participated in the first ever baseball game between Army and Navy, which was held in Annapolis, Maryland. The midshipmen razzed MacArthur with a carefully written ditty about his father. The authors made a special point to poke fun at Arthur MacArthur's attempts to capture Filipino insurgent leader, Emilio Aguinaldo:

> Are you the Governor General?
> Or a Hobo?
> Who is the boss of this show?
> You or Emilio Aguinaldo?[1]

As the dejected midshipmen learned, it was MacArthur who was boss on the field that day. He scored the winning run on a wild pitch. Years later MacArthur would recall that after the game the losing team treated him "as though I really were the governor general." Football was his favorite sport, but at 135 pounds he was too light to compete at the collegiate level. Still wishing to be part of the army football team, he opted to serve as its manager during his junior year.

While Douglas shined at West Point, his father fell into disfavor even though he was the highest-ranking officer in the army and had distinguished himself in the Philippines. Now a major general, he first commanded the Department of North Luzon and fought against the Filipino insurgents, who resented the Americans who had taken possession of the Philippines with the defeat of Spain. Eventually, MacArthur was named overall commander of the Philippines and its military governor. His forces

captured Filipino resistance leader Emilio Aguinaldo, result-
ing in the jubilant War Department's decision to prematurely
declare the Philippine-American War a success. Major General
MacArthur knew better and kept up operations against bands
of guerillas. Meanwhile, he instituted reforms such as the legal
doctrine of *habeas corpus* and a system of public education. One
historian described Major General MacArthur this way:

> Arthur in turn was much like his father, Judge MacArthur.
> The general displayed traits of versatility and nobility similar
> to his father. He excelled as a combat leader and as an adminis-
> trator, demonstrating professional excellence, fierce ambition,
> and superior intelligence in both roles. Like the judge, he had
> a keen sense of magnanimity as well as of justice. Just as his
> father became an aristocrat of the bench, General MacArthur
> became an aristocrat of the military elite—always dignified,
> usually formal, and never guilty of common officers' vices of
> excessive cussing, drinking, gambling and promiscuity.[2]

On May 5, 1900, MacArthur was appointed military governor of the Philippines and for a month he had full responsibility.
His strength in this position was cultivating the goodwill of the
Filipinos by showing them compassion and restraint. He had
no patience for officers who were cruel to the natives. And when
this occurred, which it did frequently, MacArthur called for an
investigation that occasionally led to court-martial. Sadly, his new
role was short-lived. The following month Secretary of War Elihu
Root chose William Howard Taft, a former solicitor general of

the United States and presently a federal judge, to head the five-man Philippines Commission. MacArthur was none too pleased to have the 325-pound Taft in his presence.

Although Taft tried to get along with MacArthur, the two clashed almost immediately. When Taft first arrived MacArthur refused to greet him at the Manila dock and instead sent a colonel in his place. Taft formed an early opinion of the general and wrote to Root that MacArthur seemed to be

> a very courtly, kindly man: lacking somewhat in a sense of humor; rather fond of generalizations on the psychological condition of the people; politely incredulous, and politely lacking in any great consideration for the view of anyone, as to the real situation, who is a civilian and who had been here only a comparatively short time and firmly convinced of the necessity for maintaining military etiquette in civil matters and civil government.[3]

Taft and MacArthur had a number of fundamental differences and chief among them was the former's belief that the Filipinos had been pacified and that there was no longer a need for military control. Mounting casualties among American troops suggested otherwise and MacArthur destroyed his career by suggesting that Taft butt out. Taft had the ear of Washington, MacArthur did not, and the general was called home in disgrace. Major General Adna Chafee, who came to the Philippines from China where he commanded the U.S. Relief Expedition during the Boxer Rebellion, replaced MacArthur. Thus began a distrust of military civil control that his son later adopted. Douglas often mirrored his father's disregard and scorn for civilian officials who interfered in what he considered to be his domain, especially fifty years later when he clashed with President Harry Truman.[4]

Now a commander without a command, he was insultingly relieved on the Fourth of July, though he received a hero's sendoff by his troops. MacArthur left Manila the following day and much to his disappointment his transport arrived in San Francisco in late August with only a low-ranking officer from the Department of the Pacific and a special delegation from Milwaukee at the port to greet him. Governor Taft had made sure of this. He telegraphed the White House to instruct Secretary Root not to embrace MacArthur upon his return. Taft warned that the general's "head has been swelled to such an extent that he may make a fool of himself when he reaches the United States." MacArthur didn't remain in San Francisco long. He took a train to Chicago and was greeted there by Pinky and Douglas. Arthur III, whom he saw at one point in the Philippines, was at the Naval War College in Newport, Rhode Island.

This was a turning point for Douglas MacArthur. He witnessed firsthand the shoddy treatment his father, a Medal of Honor winner, had received by the government he served so ably. From this moment forward Douglas was ingrained with a distrust of civilian leaders and their efforts to control the military. He was never able to reconcile such conduct, even as he rose through the ranks and went on to command in three wars. Time and time again Douglas clashed with his civilian superiors and eventually it would cost him his career during the Korean War.

For a time MacArthur commanded the Department of the Pacific where he was promoted to Lieutenant General. But depite the promotion MacArthur sought to resurrect his career and, after much effort, was eventually granted an audience with President William McKinley in Canton, Ohio. This was a last-gasp effort and MacArthur needed to impress upon the president that he was still a capable commander and not a washed-up old soldier. Though the meeting was initially tense, the two Civil War veterans found much in common and ended the day as friends. At that moment Taft's influence over McKinley was nothing for MacArthur to worry about. He was thousands of miles away and couldn't stand in the way of the more affable MacArthur. The general had won over the president and now had a good reason to feel optimistic about the future, but only for a very short time. Just days later McKinley traveled to Buffalo, New York, and while attending the Pan-American Exposition, he was shot. The president died of his wounds after lingering for eight days.

Graduation day at West Point, June 11, 1903, was an especially proud event for the MacArthurs. General MacArthur was granted a leave of absence from his post in San Francisco to attend the ceremony. Much to Lieutenant General MacArthur's chagrin, the person directly responsible for removing him from the Philippines, Secretary Root, was the keynote speaker. Although his rank dictated that he could sit on the rostrum near Root, the general refused and instead sat with Pinky in the audience alongside other parents. Douglas, as captain of the corps of cadets, received his diploma first. He proudly walked off the rostrum, bypassed his seat, and headed in the direction of Lieutenant

General MacArthur and Pinky. While Root likely observed the scene, Douglas reached down and handed the diploma to his beaming father.

Now a fresh second lieutenant, Douglas was given a two-month furlough and headed to San Francisco with his parents. Also nearby was Arthur III, who transferred from the Naval War College to the naval station at Mare Island, California, just outside of San Francisco. For the first time in years, the entire MacArthur family was together. In the evenings, Douglas and his brother sat by their father as he told stories about the Philippines. This was especially captivating for Douglas since he had been ordered to report there in the autumn.

That October, Lieutenant MacArthur boarded the *Sherman* and commenced his long-standing relationship with the Filipino people. His father gave him a list of contacts in Manila, but Douglas had very little time to socialize. He was assigned to the Department of the Visayas as an engineer and spent time in Panay, Samar, Cebu, and Leyte. The latter, of course, became very familiar forty years later when MacArthur came ashore there in 1944 to reclaim the Philippines.

He was immediately taken with the Philippines and the Filipino people. He was charmed by "the delightful hospitality . . . the amazingly attractive mixture of Spanish culture and American industry . . . the fun-loving men, and the moonbeam delicacy of its lovely women." And they seemed delighted with him as well.

As an engineer his work involved supervising road, bridge, and pier construction. Not only was it backbreaking work, but dangerous too. While constructing piers and docks at Guimairs Island, he led a detachment into the nearby jungle to cut timber and the party was attacked by "two of these desperadoes." What happened may have been embellished by MacArthur, but it is an exciting story and one he enjoyed recounting: "Like all frontiersmen, I was an expert with a pistol and I dropped them both dead in their tracks, but not before one had blazed away at me with his antiquated rifle. The slug tore through the top of my campaign hat and almost cut the sapling tree immediately behind me."

Lieutenant MacArthur was exposed to other guerilla activity while in the Philippines and he saw firsthand why it was the military and not civilians, as his father argued, who needed to control this dangerous region.

After less than a year he was ordered back to the United States. Upon reaching San Francisco he was assigned to low-key engineer duty at a couple of nearby posts. During one assignment at the California Debris Commission, MacArthur oversaw the excavation of mining debris that washed down into the rivers of the Sacramento and San Joaquin valleys. Thankfully the less-than-glamorous job lasted only a brief period before Lieutenant MacArthur was ordered to join his father in Japan as aide-de-camp. Lieutenant General MacArthur was observing the Russo-Japanese War. After the conflict ended in a Japanese victory, he was ordered on a China-India trip and Douglas was asked to come along.

Pinky was with her husband in Asia and now that Douglas joined them the MacArthurs were almost a full family again. During the trip they visited military bases throughout Japan and then headed to Singapore via Shanghai and Hong Kong. From there they explored all over India, and after being gone about eight months, the MacArthurs returned to Japan for another three weeks. Douglas met with some of the victorious generals and their soldiers, leaving him impressed with their "boldness and courage."

During this time, his father prepared a paper for the War Department that stressed Japan's rising military strength and the need for better defenses in the Philippines "in order to prevent its strategic position from becoming a liability rather than an asset to the United States." His prophetic words would go unheeded and the United States paid a costly price some thirty years later.

Douglas recalled the Asian trip with delight: "Traversing countless miles of lands so rich in color, so fabled in legend, so vital to history that the experience was without a doubt the most important factor of preparation in my entire life."

During the Asia trip Douglas and his father grew closer intellectually. A voracious reader, Lieutenant General MacArthur encouraged his son to purchase books on each of the countries they visited. They discussed the books each evening, as well as what they had learned that day from their visits. At his father's urging, Douglas kept a reading list throughout the trip and by the time they returned to the United States, he could accurately claim an understanding of the Asian culture, politics, and military.

The MacArthurs returned to San Francisco in August 1906 where Douglas awaited new orders while his father resumed command of the Division of the Pacific as a lieutenant general, a rank bestowed upon him by a special act of Congress before he returned from Japan. As luck would have it, Douglas was assigned to become a student at the Engineer School of Application in Washington. More importantly, however, he was assigned as aide-de-camp to President Roosevelt. The president personally requested that Douglas join his staff, probably, as one of MacArthur's biographer's surmises, "as a tribute or even a palliative to General MacArthur."[5]

Whatever the reason, Douglas was thrilled since he greatly admired the twenty-sixth president. It was Roosevelt's "vigor, courage, abounding vitality and lack of presidential pomposity" that most appealed to him. Roosevelt also thought highly of the young MacArthur, seeking his opinion on the situation in the Far East that he had witnessed firsthand.

Lieutenant General MacArthur's long military career was about to come to a close. His old nemesis, William Howard Taft, was now secretary of war and had no use for the aging soldier. The general lobbied hard to become chief of staff, but Taft wouldn't even consider it and MacArthur spent his last years in the army a bitter man. He moved back to Milwaukee to live in a rented house with Pinky and spent his days writing reports on the Russo-Japanese War and his trip to Asia. Pinky was bored in Milwaukee, but mostly she missed her favorite son, Douglas. She cajoled her husband to use what little influence he had left to get the younger MacArthur reassigned as an engineer of rivers and harbors in Milwaukee. Much to his mother's delight, Douglas moved in with his parents and in the evening he and his father discussed politics, history, literature, and a topic of great interest to both of them, Asia.

As always Douglas was enthralled by his father's stories about the Filipino people and he could relate, having just spent time in the Philippines. Sadly, he also learned about the harsh realities of army life and how civilians and military officers didn't always see eye to eye. His father's poor attitude about the U.S. Army may have rubbed off on Douglas at this time. He was neglecting his engineering duties and, for the first time in his young career, this resulted in a poor efficiency rating. His commanding officer, Major William V. Judson, wrote that Lieutenant MacArthur "exhibited less interest in and put less time upon the drafting room, the plans and specifications for work." No doubt his assignment was less than stimulating in the Philippines and boredom set in. Also, Douglas was spending more time than he should have courting Fanniebelle Stuart, a local beauty who hardly reciprocated his romantic yearnings.

General MacArthur knew Milwaukee was no place for his son if he wanted to progress within the army, so he saw to it that Douglas was transferred to Fort Leavenworth as commander of Company K and as instructor at the Fort Riley's Mounted Service School. Pinky was crushed. Mother and son had always had a strong bond and they had grown even closer during the Asia trip and during his time in Milwaukee. She missed his company so much that she tried to coerce him back by securing a job from the owner of Union Pacific Railroad. Douglas, wisely, refused.

In 1911, Lieutenant MacArthur was ordered to San Antonio to serve with the so-called Maneuver Division, a composite unit formed on the Mexican border to ease tensions there. For MacArthur it was a homecoming. The assignment allowed him to return to the West Texas Military Academy campus where he had played sports. On a visit to the campus, students gawked at MacArthur—not because he was one of the school's first graduates but because of the army regulation hat he wore, known as a "Montana Peak." Jutted skyward into what he called a "nondescript sort of pyramid." The cadets mocked and jeered.

Later that night he had another rude awakening. While strolling around the home he had lived in with his family, MacArthur was startled by a young woman who demanded to know what he was doing there. Before he could give a proper answer, the woman declared that MacArthur was drunk and told him to "get out or I will call the guard." Even though the division camped nearby for four months, MacArthur was so stunned by the episode he never attempted to return. MacArthur later wrote: "I had learned one of the bitter lessons of life, never try to regain the past; the fire will have become ashes."[6]

Two years before, on June 2, 1909, Arthur MacArthur reached mandatory retirement age and, after serving forty-seven years, departed the army with no ceremony or farewell address. He spent his days enjoying the library he had amassed, gave occasional speeches to veterans' organizations, and commenced work on his memoirs. Slowly his health deteriorated; he suffered from indigestion, high blood pressure, and kidney problems.

On September 5, 1912, while attending the fiftieth reunion of the 24th Wisconsin Volunteers at Walcott Hall, Lieutenant General MacArthur collapsed on the dais as he regaled the old veterans with stories of the 24th's exploits during the Civil War. His doctor was in attendance and rushed to assist the general.

MacArthur was moved to a more comfortable spot where he could be examined. The doctor looked up after a few moments and announced to the shocked crowd what they already suspected: Arthur MacArthur was dead. Many of them began sobbing and, in between the tears, one old veteran began to recite the Lord's Prayer. Eventually everyone joined him. In a final tribute to MacArthur's storied career, another veteran removed a flag from the wall and placed it over the general's body.[7]

Pinky, devastated at the news, immediately alerted her sons to return home. Arthur III and Douglas arrived in Milwaukee two days later. Douglas was never the same after losing his father. He said: "My whole world changed that night. Never have I been able to heal the wound in my heart."[8] The funeral was modest, just as Lieutenant General MacArthur had wanted. A private service, directed by the Reverend Paul B. Jenkins, was held at the family residence attended by his closest friends and family. The pastor of Immanuel Church read brief selections from the Scriptures and then a William Wordsworth poem, "The Happy Warrior." At the general's request, he was not buried in Arlington Cemetery, but laid to rest in Milwaukee's Forest Lawn Cemetery. Douglas had his remains reinterred twenty years later when Pinky died, and the two are buried next to each other in Arlington.

FOUR

The Making of a Hero

AFTER HIS FATHER'S death, Douglas was reassigned from Fort Leavenworth to the Engineer Board in Washington. Pinky also moved with him. Her health was deteriorating and she needed someone to watch over her. Washington was good to MacArthur. He was selected as a member of the General Board and the assignment afforded him the chance to associate with senior army and navy officers. Heading the board was army Chief of Staff Leonard Wood. MacArthur had met him as little boy on the frontier when Wood and MacArthur's father were young captains. Wood won the Medal of Honor for his service then and was considered one of the army's greater minds. During the Spanish-American War he formed the Rough Riders with Theodore Roosevelt and took the unit to Cuba—though

Wood contracted yellow fever leaving Roosevelt to win glory during an attack on the San Juan Heights.

MacArthur's tenure under Wood proved invaluable. He served as the chief of staff's assistant and spent long days working on military preparedness. Wood is considered an innovator in this area and his summer Plattsburgh Camps for officers in 1916 turned into the later Reserve Officers Training Corps (ROTC). MacArthur worked long hours in the General Staff office and he developed a regimen for staying late that continued for the next fifty years.

Far to the south, relations between the United States and Mexico were falling apart. By 1914 a new government in Mexico under General Victoriano Huerta was blamed for committing numerous atrocities, as well as threatening American interests in his country. President Woodrow Wilson uncharacteristically flexed his muscles by ordering a blockade of the port of Veracruz by the navy, and eventually American sailors and Marines seized the city. But they were too few in number to have much of an impact and if the United States was going to make a stand, a larger force was needed. Huerta did not take Wilson seriously and it now appeared that the two countries might go to war again. Secretary of War Lindley M. Garrison ordered Wood to form a small expeditionary force and ready it for Veracruz. Immediately, Wood sent MacArthur with an intelligence agent on a reconnaissance mission to "study the lay of the land, and observe and report on all matters."[1]

This was an exciting task for MacArthur. It took him away from his desk job and he made the most of the assignment.

Right away he saw that a lack of transportation within the city would hamper movement of troops and supplies. As he explored Veracruz he noticed some nearby freight and passenger cars, but none were attached to locomotives. Eager to solve this predicament, MacArthur was told by a drunken Mexican engineer that locomotives could be found about forty miles away in the town of Alvarado. He sobered up his new friend with a bribe of $150 and the two of them went looking for the locomotives. It was a dangerous mission and MacArthur probably should not have undertaken it on his own, but the only other U.S. soldiers at hand were the 4th Infantry Regiment. Its commander, Captain Constant Cordier, had to stay with his troops. So MacArthur and the engineer traveled southeast to Alvarado by handcar and with the help of two other Mexicans they found three locomotives.

On the way back to Veracruz the party ran into trouble. MacArthur, armed with a 38-caliber revolver, was the only one with a weapon when five Mexican bandits accosted them. Three of the men left without incident, but two of the rebels tried to pick a fight with MacArthur and he was "obliged to fire upon them." Farther north the party met with yet more resistance, and MacArthur shot four rebels at Piedra and another one at Laguna. Eventually they made it back to the American lines with the Mexicans engineering the three locomotives while MacArthur was transported by a combination of handcar, boat, and pony. He reported the events to Cordier, who then forwarded the details on to Wood. This was the only engagement between Americans and Mexicans during the entire Veracruz expedition.

MacArthur remained at Veracruz just a few weeks longer

before returning to General Staff duty in Washington. Wood was impressed by MacArthur's courage in retrieving the locomotives and recommended him for the Medal of Honor. Wood's recommendation told how MacArthur had made the trip "on his own initiative and at the risk of his life and this indicates an amount of enterprise and courage worthy of high commendation." A board was appointed to consider the application and concluded there was no "incontestable proof" of the incident since MacArthur had written the only firsthand report. They furthermore stated that he had been more reckless than heroic.

Being refused the medal that had been awarded to his father was a blow to MacArthur's ego. He later protested with a letter to Major General Hugh Scott, the new chief of staff. MacArthur accused the board of "rigid narrow-mindedness and a lack of imagination." This was unwise but typical of MacArthur's vanity and fire. As a biographer pointed out: "A pattern of behavior was becoming increasingly evident in him, [which] branded MacArthur in the eyes of many officers as a pleader for special consideration and a sensitive, self-righteous protester against any infringements upon which he felt were his prerogatives."[2]

Years later MacArthur reevaluated the whole affair when he said: "In deciding to make the reconnaissance I may have been right or I may have been wrong. War did not materialize and the utility of our exploits would never be known, but even my old frontier friends would have agreed that it was a wild night under the Southern Cross."

Yet his self-promotion had no impact on his career path. By 1916 he was promoted to major and worked on drafting national defense legislation. For a brief period he was the superintendent of the War and State Building that sits next to the White House and is now called the Old Executive Building. While he was out of harm's way in Washington, the rest of the world was in turmoil. Since August 1914, Europe had been embroiled in what eventually became known as the First World War. Meanwhile, the United States and Mexico were at each other's throats again. This time it was over a ten-thousand-man punitive expedition led by Brigadier General John J. Pershing in search of bandit leader Pancho Villa, who in March 1916 raided a U.S. garrison in Columbus, New Mexico.

MacArthur spent his days in Washington courting legislators, particularly Republican congressman Julius Kahn, a ranking member of the House Military Affairs Committee. MacArthur wanted Congress to double the size of the 220,000-man regular army, but even twice that strength would not be sufficient in the likelihood the United States entered the conflict in Europe. He was making a name for himself among the country's lawmakers and this caught the attention of Secretary of War Newton D. Baker, former mayor of Cleveland and a journalist. MacArthur and Baker spent a lot of time together with the former "trying to match his [Baker's] swift and uninhibited mind, and answer the innumerable questions of a purely military nature that were constantly popping up."[3]

Because of his background, Baker wanted to improve the War Department's relationship with the press. This led to the creation of the Bureau of Information with MacArthur in charge. MacArthur and the press got on well despite his conviction that in the event of war a strict censorship policy should be put in place to not only deter the leaking of military secrets but also to prevent biased or inaccurate reporting. He enjoyed his new job and told his old friend Leonard Wood, "I am working very hard with my newspaper men."[4] MacArthur, like his grandfather, found Washington a hospitable place. He and Pinky resided at the Ontario, one of the city's most elite apartment buildings. Status was important to him and for the remainder of his life he lived in luxury whenever possible.

By early 1917, the United States crept closer to joining the world war. Two years earlier a German U-boat had sunk the *Lusitania* and 128 Americans perished. Germany then announced unrestricted submarine warfare, which meant any European-bound American merchant vessel was fair game. American public opinion now shifted in favor of the United States joining the war, but Wilson was not yet among them. It took the Zimmerman telegram, a proposal from Germany to Mexico to make war against the United States, to eventually push Wilson into sending American troops to fight overseas.

Meanwhile, the General Staff prepared for the conflict by planning how the military would mobilize when the time came. On February 19, 1917, the army was thrown into chaos. Major General Frederick Funston, who commanded the Southern Department at Fort Sam Houston, Texas, dropped dead of a heart attack. He was considered the army's most experienced commander and a sure bet to lead American forces in France when the time came. MacArthur was working late in the General Staff office when the telegram announcing Funston's death arrived.

Anticipating that his boss would want to hear about Funston immediately, MacArthur went to Baker's home where the secretary of war was hosting a dinner for President Wilson. At first MacArthur was denied entrance, but he pushed his way past the butler and this drew Wilson's attention, who said: "Come in, Major, and tell us all the news. There are no secrets here." MacArthur did just that. Wilson was silent for a moment and then inquired of Baker, "Who will take over the army now?"

The secretary had no response and looked to MacArthur for the answer. MacArthur responded, either John J. Pershing or Peyton March. As history showed, Pershing was selected and soon commanded the American Expeditionary Forces (AEF) after President Wilson went before Congress on April 4, 1917, and received a declaration of war against Germany. Pershing was the correct choice. Although he lacked combat experience, as did Scott for that matter, Pershing proved capable when dealing with the difficult British and French commanders in how to best utilize the American forces on the Western Front.

MacArthur vividly recalled the first time he met Pershing. Just days after graduating from West Point, MacArthur was in his father's office in downtown San Francisco when Captain Pershing, then a cavalry officer, came by for a visit. "I shall never forget the impression he made on me by his appearance and bearing," MacArthur reminisced. "He was the very epitome of what is now affectionately called the 'Old Army.'" When Pershing turned to leave he told Arthur MacArthur, "I am sure Douglas and I will meet again." Pershing could not have been more correct. Their paths crossed often when Douglas served in Washington, and in many ways Douglas modeled his career after Pershing's. Their interaction increased over the next year and a half when Major MacArthur played a significant role in the AEF.

A true warrior, MacArthur wanted to fight in the Great War and in early summer 1917 expended all his energy trying to make this happen. Not interested in remaining on the General Staff while preparing others for the great battles ahead, MacArthur wanted to be in the thick of it, just like his father. One way was to align himself with the National Guard, which was surely going to be needed overseas. It didn't matter that most regular officers hated the Guard units. They were deemed part-time soldiers who were poorly led and poorly trained. There were exceptions. Some of the New York units were as good as any regular regiment, but by and large the stereotype was correct. Perhaps what they needed most were experienced officers like MacArthur to whip them into shape.

National Guard units were also very political and closely aligned with Congress. Like the regular regiments, all of the state units were to be formed into divisions of almost twenty-eight thousand officers and men. The AEF would also consist of drafted troops. Since there were so many state units at the War Department's disposal and not all of them could possibly fit into the army's tables of organization, MacArthur came up with the idea of drawing the excess units together to form a composite division. He envisioned units "that will stretch over the whole country like a rainbow." Thus MacArthur's creation was called the Rainbow Division. He allied with Major General William A. Mann, the head of the Militia Bureau and the most experienced of any officer when it came to the National Guard, to determine which units were available and present the plan to the War Department.

Secretary of War Baker liked MacArthur's idea and on August 1, 1917, he put the plan into action. The 42nd Rainbow Division was born. Then Baker promoted Major MacArthur to colonel and gave him the option of remaining in the engineers or transferring to the infantry. MacArthur said he chose the latter because "I could think only of the old 24th Wisconsin Infantry." His father's influence always seemed to be at the forefront of Douglas's career decisions. The sixty-three-year-old Mann was chosen to command the 42nd Division and he appointed MacArthur as his chief of staff.

MacArthur confers with the staff of the 42nd "Rainbow" Division (1918).

General John J. Pershing, commander of the American Expeditionary Forces, pins the Distinguish Service Cross on MacArthur for his bravery on the Chateau-Thierry Front (1918).

MacArthur stands in front of his car at St. Juvin, France (1918).

FIVE

Going to War with the Rainbow Division

THE RAINBOW DIVISION took shape at Camp Albert L. Mills on Hampstead Plains, near Garden City, Long Island. Named for the superintendant of West Point while MacArthur was a cadet, the temporary camp was some twenty miles from New York City. Units from twenty-six states began arriving in early August, though it would take six weeks before the Rainbow was at full strength. Tables of organization dictated that all AEF combat divisions would consist of two infantry brigades and one artillery brigade, plus various medical, signal, military police, and administrative support units. Major General Mann, Brigadier General Charles P. Summerall—who commanded the artillery brigade—and MacArthur poured over lists of National Guard units seeking out those with established records of efficiency, while making sure the outfits selected came from as many states as possible.

It was MacArthur's responsibility to assure that all of the units received the "sound basic principles which for time immemorial have laid the solid foundations for victory."[1] This meant drilling, both elementary and close order, and plenty of reviews. Rifle practice, at the insistence of General Pershing, was also stressed. Pershing's observers on the Western Front convinced him that it was "highly important infantry soldiers should be excellent shots."[2]

Because the 42nd was earmarked as one of the early divisions to head overseas, it completed training in less than three months—most divisions trained two or three times longer. Besides organizing the divisional training, MacArthur was busy trying to outfit and supply his men. Basic essentials such as underwear, woolen clothing, and shelter halves were hard to come by, even though War Department contractors worked around the clock to fill quartermaster depots.

Like most of the army training facilities in 1917, Camp Mills was newly established and construction of the barracks was not completed when the men arrived. They had to sleep outdoors, but there weren't even enough tents to go around. In some cases twelve men slept in one tent when the tents were designed to hold half that many. At the end of September, Secretary of War Baker, his new chief of staff, Major General Tasker H. Bliss, as well as other high-ranking officers reviewed the division. Afterward the division was given high marks despite the fact that two regiments almost collided during the parade, some soldiers saluted when given the "eyes right" command, and a few officers were cited for improper attire. MacArthur was embarrassed and made this known in a circular sent to all commanding officers.

Then on October 18, 1917, the division left Camp Mills, and made the short journey to the port of embarkation at Hoboken, New Jersey, in preparation for sailing overseas. The following day they left for Saint-Nazaire, France. MacArthur journeyed onboard the army transport *Covington*. Only months before the vessel had been the Hamburg American liner *Cincinnati*, but it had been seized in American waters along with other German ships after war was declared. The journey took two weeks and each day the men of the Rainbow Division were brought up on deck to drill and exercise.

There was constant fear of German U-boat attacks so all aboard wore lifebelts and stayed near the life rafts hanging on the side of the ships. To discourage attack, navy escorts surrounded the ship in a convoy and used a zigzag pattern to throw off enemy submarines. One of the escort ships was the *Chattanooga*, commanded by Captain Arthur MacArthur. Knowing his brother was in the same water gave Douglas "a glow in his heart." After safely disembarking the 42nd Division in France on November 1, 1917, the *Covington* was sunk on its way back to the United States.

Shortly after arriving at Saint-Nazaire, MacArthur headed to Vaucouleurs in the Lorraine Valley, where the division set up headquarters for a short period. It was a quiet sector and the Rainbow was there to train. Soon afterward Pershing visited the

division and concluded that its frail, sixty-three-year-old commander had no business leading twenty-eight thousand officers
and men in the hazardous trenches of the Western Front. Mann
was close to retirement and Pershing was going to help him reach
that milestone, but not in France. In late December Mann was
sent back to the United States to command the Department of
East before retiring in 1918.

Meanwhile MacArthur busied himself by putting the division through a steady training regimen despite almost constant
rain. This could have turned out to be a waste of time because
the 42nd learned it was to disband and its units were to become
replacements for an American corps of three divisions that
Pershing wanted to form. Mann protested that the Rainbow was
an important element of the AEF and its elimination would be
disastrous. It was to no avail since he was on his way out and
Pershing paid no attention to him. Mann had powerful friends in
Washington, however, whom he knew from his days as chief of
militia. He teamed up with MacArthur and they bombarded his
connections in the United States with cablegrams pleading for
help to keep the Rainbow intact. They, in turn, called and wrote
to the War Department on behalf of the 42nd Division.

MacArthur was not willing to wait and see what happened.
He went over Mann's head and visited Pershing's Chaumont
headquarters to see an old acquaintance from the Philippines,
Brigadier General James J. Harbord, who was now AEF chief of
staff. MacArthur "asked him to come and see the division and
judge for himself on the merits of the situation whether such
a splendid unit should be relegated to a replacement status."

Harbord agreed, saw that MacArthur was correct, and revoked the order. MacArthur's bold move sent shockwaves through Pershing's staff, but this was his manner: to do what he felt was right and in his best interest.

In February 1918 the division was placed in a combat sector in the Lunéville-Baccarat area to train with four experienced French infantry regiments under the command of General Georges de Bazelaire. Mann, whose poor health continued to deteriorate, was replaced as division commander by Major General Charles T. Menoher, a regular colonel in the field artillery and a former West Point classmate of Pershing's. MacArthur liked him a great deal, calling Menoher "an able officer, an efficient administrator, of genial disposition and unimpeachable character."[3] MacArthur especially appreciated the fact that he preferred to command from behind the lines and allowed his chief of staff to go to the front. The two became great friends and during the Korean War Menoher's son was one of MacArthur's assistant division commanders.

MacArthur's first action against the enemy occurred on February 26, 1918. Eager to test his mettle as his father had done on the battlefields of the Civil War, MacArthur organized a raiding party. He told Bazelaire, "I cannot fight them [the Germans] if I cannot see them." That night the party crawled through no-man's-land. When battlefield debris slowed them down, they were spotted by a German soldier guarding the outermost trenches directly in front of them. The guard discharged his gun at MacArthur's party and was soon joined by other Germans who fired machine guns and an artillery barrage.

Now trapped, MacArthur and the raiders had no choice but to fight. They dove into the trenches and hand-to-hand combat ensued. The affair ended when one of the French soldiers threw a grenade into a German dugout, forcing the survivors to surrender. MacArthur and the French returned to the rear with several German prisoners where they were greeted with cheers, cognac, and absinthe. The French soldiers were so impressed by MacArthur's bravery that Bazelaire pinned a Croix de Guerre on his tunic and kissed him on both cheeks. Not to be upstaged, the American Army awarded MacArthur the Silver Star for "extraordinary heroism and gallantry in action."

Not only had MacArthur made a name for himself as a brave soldier, but as a stylish dresser too. He removed the metal band from the inside of his cap, which gave the headpiece a jaunty appearance. The damp French autumn climate was perfect for the heavy muffler and bright turtleneck sweater he favored, and he was rarely seen without a riding crop and shining puttees. He wore such attire while behind the lines and at the front with his troops, earning nicknames such as "the Dude," "the Stick," and "Beau Brummell of the AEF," among others.[4]

Feeling confident on the battlefield, MacArthur received permission in early March to accompany a battalion from the 168th Infantry during a much larger raid on a German trench occupying the Salient du Feyes. With the operation to commence just after 5:00 a.m., French artillery moved into position five minutes earlier to lay down a supporting barrage. It was a cold, drizzly morning and the ground was ankle-deep in mud. Before the French guns could fire off a round, the Germans somehow knew what was happening and aimed their artillery at the stunned Americans with deadly accuracy.

As casualties mounted MacArthur walked the line to reassure the men. Then right on schedule the French guns blasted away toward the Germans. Ten minutes later a company battalion commander received the "all ready" order from MacArthur and blew his whistle. Even with the deafening noise MacArthur could still hear the commander encourage his men as they climbed out of the trench: "Keep alignment, Guide is right. Don't rush or you'll get your own barrage on your neck."

Caught up in the drama, MacArthur recalled, "I went over the top as fast as I could and scrambled forward. The blast was like a fiery furnace." At first MacArthur thought he was by himself until suddenly he saw that his men "were around me, ahead of me, roaring avalanche of glittering steel and cursing men." They carried the day, just as Arthur MacArthur had done so often in the Civil War. Douglas MacArthur was again recognized for his bravery and received yet another medal. This time it was the Distinguished Service Cross, second only to the Medal of Honor.

For the next three months the 42nd held the Baccarat sector by itself, the only AEF division to occupy a sector on its own. Although the Rainbow was supposed to spend this time training, most of their time was spent conducting raids and patrols. MacArthur said that "for eighty-two days the division was in almost constant combat." Then, in June, the division was ordered to take part in what became known as the Champagne-Marne operation. While making preparations for the move, General Pershing again visited the 42nd. The AEF commander was none too pleased at what he perceived was a poorly disciplined and not properly trained division. He directed his comments at MacArthur who had little to say in response. In reality the Rainbow was one of the most experienced and best divisions in the AEF and Pershing's observations were simply wrong.

Much to his surprise, MacArthur was notified five days after Pershing's tirade that he was promoted to brigadier general. Little did he know that Pinky had written Pershing what she called "a little heart-to-heart letter" that touted her son's extraordinary accomplishments. Pinky then tugged at Pershing's heartstrings by telling him, "My hope and ambition in life is to live long enough to see this son made a General Officer, and I feel I am placing my entire life, as it were, in your hands for consideration."[5] After Douglas accepted the commission as brigadier general, Pershing wrote Pinky a letter of congratulations. Brigadier General MacArthur had become the most famous member of the Rainbow, better known than poet Joyce Kilmer and chaplain Father Duffy, who also served in the division.

Upon arrival in the vicinity of Châlons-sur-Marne, the Rainbow was placed in the reserve of the French Fourth Army where it remained until joining Major General Hunter Liggett's I Corps, attached to the French Sixth Army in the vicinity of Chateau Thierry. There, with MacArthur again at the front, the 42nd was ordered to pursue German units positioned on rugged slopes and in dense woods surrounding the town. For six days the 42nd Division and German units slugged it out during several close action battles that consisted of attacks and counterattacks from both sides. Then, reminiscent of his father's action at

Missionary Ridge, the infantry of the 42nd charged up the slopes and seized Hill 184. But the fight wasn't over. MacArthur could hear the Germans abandoning their position nearby and ordered one of his regiments to move forward with one battalion, followed by a second in support and a third in reserve.

Without consulting Menoher or Liggett, MacArthur called for an artillery barrage as protection and in the early morning of July 30 his infantry prepared for battle. MacArthur recalled that as they traversed through the German lines the "dead were so thick in spots we tumbled over them . . . and the moans and cries of wounded men sounded everywhere."[6] By the end of the day MacArthur's men had cleared out all the remaining German positions and he returned to the rear and explained to Hunter and Menoher what had occurred. For this action MacArthur received another Silver Star. He would ultimately receive five of these decorations during the war. Menoher called him "the bloodiest fighting man in this army."[7] During eight days of action near the Ourcq and Vesle rivers, the 42nd had suffered fifty-five hundred casualties, among them the famed poet Sergeant Joyce Kilmer, who was killed on July 30.

Although he relished the accolades bestowed upon him, MacArthur also recognized that such heroism came with a cost. A week after the victory he joined a group of fellow officers at a bar for a rare evening of drinking and carousing, but he could not seem to enjoy himself. "I found something missing," he wrote. "It may have been the vision of those writhing bodies hanging from the barbed wire or the stench of dead flesh still in my nostrils. Perhaps I was just getting old: somehow I forgot how to play."[8]

As a young boy on the frontier he had pretended to be a cowboy fighting Indians, but now this was all too real.

There was little time to reflect on the previous battle because on September 12, 1918, MacArthur and the rest of Pershing's newly formed First Army were about to get their biggest test of the war. Up until this point, every battle in which the AEF was engaged had been fought as part of the Allied armies, either the British or the French. Pershing was anxious to see if his doughboys could fight alone, and he pushed the supreme commander of the Allied Forces, General Ferdinand Foch, to allow the Americans to attack the St. Mihiel Salient. It was a bulge in the Allied lines twenty-five miles wide and fifteen miles deep, which the Germans had occupied for four years.

Foch reluctantly gave Pershing the go-ahead and the Rainbow was placed in the center of the line and ordered to lead the attack. At 1:00 a.m. on the twelfth, division artillery blasted the German position for four hours. As dawn broke MacArthur's brigade jumped off, followed by a tank brigade led by Lieutenant Colonel George Patton. The tanks were of little use because they got stuck in the heavy mud, but MacArthur's infantry fared much better. By nightfall the 42nd had captured the village of Essey and liberated its inhabitants of old men, women, and children from German occupation. For this action MacArthur received his fifth Silver Star.[9]

The St. Mihiel offensive was a huge success and morale booster for the AEF, particularly for Pershing. It showed the other Allied commanders, who were beginning to have doubts about the American soldiers' ability to fight on the Western Front and the capabilities of its commanders to lead them, that indeed

Pershing's doughboys were as good as any soldier on the battle-fields of France. But in reality the Germans were in the process of abandoning the salient and didn't put up much of a fight. In fact, "*Kamerad!*" (German for *comrade*) was frequently shouted by tired German soldiers who simply wanted to give up. The elated doughboys were happy to accommodate. In just a few days they proudly rounded up several hundred prisoners and sent them to the rear to wait out the war.

A dramatic moment occurred during the St. Mihiel offensive when MacArthur and Patton met for the first time on a hill overlooking Essey. MacArthur was sporting his barracks cap and a scarf his mother had knitted for him, while Patton had an ivory-handled Colt .45 on his hip. It is not known what the two West Point graduates and future heroes of World War II said to each other. In *Reminiscences*, MacArthur only mentions Patton in passing and incorrectly identifies him as a lieutenant colonel. Patton, on the other hand, referred to the meeting in a letter to his wife:

> I met General MacArthur commanding a brigade, he was walking about too. I joined him and the creeping barrage came along towards us, but it was very thin and not dangerous. I think each one wanted to leave but each hated to say so, so we let it come over us. We stood and talked but neither was much interested in what the other said as we could not get our minds off the shells.[10]

MacArthur had wanted to advance beyond Essey to try and take the city of Metz. He made his case to the division, corps, and army commanders and they all agreed with him that taking the fortress city might bring the war to a quick conclusion. Afterward he went to Chaumont where Pershing had the final say, and his answer was a resounding no. Pershing's main reason was that preparations were under way for a much larger operation in the Meuse-Argonne region.

SIX

The Final Offensive

ONLY TWO WEEKS after the St. Mihiel salient was cleared, five hundred thousand AEF soldiers shifted sixty miles to the east into the Meuse-Argonne region, so-called for the Meuse River and the Argonne Forest. Pershing's main objective was the important Sedan-Mezieres-Carnigan railroad line, which was vital to the German communication system. Getting to it would not be easy and involved breaking through a portion of the Hindenburg Line that was heavily fortified with machine-gun nests, concrete pillboxes, and barbed wire. A central feature in this part of the line was the Romagne Heights and this was Pershing's main object for the first day of the operation, set for September 26, 1918.

Although the 42nd Division was not involved in the initial attack, it stayed close to St. Mihiel in an area called the

Essey-Pannes sector. Close by were some small German units who never left the salient. They made things interesting for the Rainbow troops with frequent raids, airplane bombardments, and artillery fire. MacArthur took an old chateau at St. Benoit as his headquarters, but shortly thereafter learned he was being evicted. A group of Germans captured in a recent raid bragged that the structure was a target for their army's heavy guns. Sure enough, within hours a barrage destroyed the old house.

Pershing's headquarters sent orders for the 42nd, and other divisions holding the front northeast of St. Mihiel, to make deep raids—as a diversionary measure—at the same time the Meuse-Argonne offensive was to commence. MacArthur devised a plan for an elaborate double raid that sent his infantry regiments against German positions at Marimbois Farm and Haumont. Artillery fire prior to the raids "was so accurate and over-whelming," MacArthur said, "that both German garrisons were practically annihilated." Undeterred, the Germans who survived the barrage resisted the Americans with heavy machine-gun fire and afterward it is doubtful the raids had any diversionary impact on the main attack. As usual MacArthur went forward with his men and earned his sixth Silver Star.

One week later the 42nd was ordered to the Meuse-Argonne region and placed in the reserve area of the American V Corps near Montfaucon Woods. This time MacArthur's headquarters was a rain-soaked dugout he shared with numerous broken tree limbs, the result of German artillery. Currently there was a lull in the fighting and Pershing reorganized the AEF, which had fallen apart just days into the offensive. He relinquished command of the First Army to Hunter Liggett, formed Second Army, and appointed several new corps commanders. Charles P. Summerall was one of them. Formally in command of the 42nd Division artillery brigade, then 1st Division commander, he now headed V Corps and was happy to have the 42nd Division with him.

On the night of October 11 the fighting resumed and the 42nd entered the line running from the town of Sommerance eastward through the northern edge of the Romagne Woods. In the ensuing days the division's line extended and it was becoming more and more obvious that the Rainbow was about to take part in a major operation.

Looming in front of MacArthur and the 42nd Division were two strong points of the fortified Kriemehelde Stellung, as this section of the Hindenburg Line was known. They were Hill 288 and the Cote de Châttïllon and the Rainbow was tasked with taking both. MacArthur's headquarters were now much improved from the cold, wet dugout. He occupied a farm east of Exermont that was two miles from the front, but still within easy range of German artillery. MacArthur had a bad habit of visiting the front without a gas mask and on one of his reconnaissance missions he was caught in Yperite gas barrage and became violently ill. It was suggested that he might need to be hospitalized, but MacArthur insisted he remain close at hand to lead the troops when the battle commenced. He said that as a result of the gas attack "he was wounded, but not incapacitated, and was able to continue functioning."[1] He was awarded the Purple Heart for this injury.

MacArthur's forays to the front gave him firsthand exposure to the danger his men would face when they attacked the Cote de Châttillon. First, the attack would require traversing across open ground toward heavy German machine-gun fire. He worried about the attack and confessed to Menoher that "he was not certain" his men could take the position. The attack was set for October 14. The evening before, Summerall paid a visit to MacArthur's headquarters. The corps commander did not mince words and told MacArthur: "Give me Châttillon, or a list of five thousand casualties." MacArthur, also never at a loss for words, responded: "If this Brigade does not capture Châttillon you can publish a casualty list of the entire Brigade with the Brigade Commander's name at the top."[2]

For a brief moment emotion overtook the two soldiers. Both had helped form the Rainbow and now the division was about to undertake its most difficult operation of the war. After MacArthur made his declaration, "tears sprang into General Summerall's eyes. He was evidently so moved he could say nothing. He looked at me for a few seconds and then left without a word." It is likely that MacArthur and the men in his brigade slept poorly that night. Not only did German artillery pound the American positions well into the morning, but also a constant rain probably made rest nearly impossible.

At 8:00 a.m. the Rainbow jumped off with support of a rolling barrage. The 83rd Brigade was in the lead and at first encountered light resistance, but that didn't last. Heavy machine-gun fire from the front and both flanks halted the brigade about a mile from their first objective. MacArthur's 84th Brigade also met heavy fire from the entrenched enemy, but his regiments kept fighting on and captured the crest of Hill 288.

Most of the Germans were killed, although about one hundred surrendered.

All of the battles were costly for MacArthur's brigade, but this particular fight was especially bloody. Casualties mounted and the sanitary train found it difficult to transport wounded doughboys to the rear because a lack of roads made ambulances useless, so they resorted to mules and hand litters. Heavy losses notwithstanding, the objective of the Cote de Châttïllon had not been met and the 42nd had to try again the next day, which they did with the same result. Summerall lost patience and took it out on the 83rd Brigade commander, Brigadier General Michael J. Lenihan. He was relieved and MacArthur could easily have been fired too, but Summerall gave him until 6:00 p.m. October 26 to take the Cote de Châttïllon. MacArthur assured him it would be done. He met with his battalion and regimental commanders and they devised a plan to send one battalion around the rear, then others would attack the front. It was their only hope in the desperate situation.

The twenty-sixth was another brutal day of fighting, but this time the outcome was different. Châttïllon was captured and held against German counterattacks. A satisfied MacArthur said that "officers fell and sergeants leaped into the command. Companies dwindled to platoons and corporals took over."[3] Summerall was so pleased to hear the great news that he put MacArthur in for the Medal of Honor and a promotion to major general, but Pershing's headquarters said no to both. He was, however, awarded his second Distinguished Service Cross. The citation read that MacArthur "displayed indomitable resolution and great courage in rallying broken lines and reforming attacks, thereby making victory possible. On a field where courage was the rule, his courage was the dominant factor."

For now the Rainbow remained at the front to consolidate its position and form a defensive line. A tally of casualties during the past few days determined they had lost four thousand killed or wounded. The next phase of the offensive was set for November 1 and the division expected to play a major role. Three days later, on the night of November 4, the Rainbow relieved the 78th Division twelve miles below Sedan. By now the Germans were falling back to the Meuse and the historic city that held great significance. The French had lost Sedan to the Germans in 1870 during the Franco-Prussian War and symbolically it was important for their army to take back the city in 1918.

French pride notwithstanding, Pershing wanted the Americans to enter the city first and made his wishes known to the corps commanders by way of AEF operations officer, Colonel George C. Marshall. However, Marshall sent confusing instructions: "General Pershing desires that the honor of entering Sedan should fall to the American First Army." Although this part of the message was clear, the second part was not: "Your attention is invited to favorable opportunity now existing for pressing our advance through the night. Boundaries will not be considered binding."

Sedan was only three miles in front of MacArthur's troops and he could likely reach the city within a day if German resistance was light. He didn't know that Summerall had told the 1st Division they were to take Sedan and this meant they were on a collision course with the 42nd. Luckily MacArthur conferred with Menoher and the two agreed that their push should be made the following day when it was light out and afforded greater opportunity for success.

What happened next is one of the more bizarre events of the war. That night MacArthur was awakened and told that the 42nd Division was being infiltrated by unknown troops and an altercation was about to take place. He dressed and headed to the front. There he stopped to read a map and was confronted by a 16th Infantry Regiment patrol led by a Lieutenant Black. MacArthur was wearing his trademark floppy hat, muffler, riding breeches, and polished boots and to the lieutenant he looked like a German.

MacArthur was taken prisoner at gunpoint, but they quickly released him with apologies after he revealed his identity. MacArthur later detailed why he was often seen carrying non-regulation equipment and insisted on leading from the front:

> I fought from the front as I could not effectively manipulate my troops from the rear: I wore no helmet because it hurt my head. I carried no gas mask because it hampered my movements. I went unarmed because it was not my purpose to engage in personal combat, but to direct others. I used a riding crop out of long habit on the plains.[4]

Meanwhile the 1st Division withdrew from the 42nd sector, the Rainbow was relieved, and the French took Sedan after all.

On November 6, 1918, MacArthur took over the division when Menoher was appointed corps commander. It was a proud moment for him and his mother, who learned firsthand of her son's exploits from a letter Menoher wrote to Pershing that was copied by him and sent to Pinky.

[MacArthur] is the bloodiest fighting man in this army. I'm afraid we're going to lose him sometime, for there's no risk of battle any soldier is called upon to take that he is not liable to look up and see MacArthur at his side. At every advance MacArthur, with just his cap and riding crop, will go forward with the first line. He is the source of the greatest possible inspiration to the men of this division who are devoted to him. [5]

Pershing took Menoher at his word and recommended MacArthur for a second star. But the chief of staff, Major General Peyton March, froze all promotions and a disappointed MacArthur was denied a promotion to major general. On November 22 Major General Clement Flagler took command of the division and MacArthur returned to the 84th Division. One of Flagler's first acts was to put MacArthur in for the Medal of Honor: "For most distinguished gallantry in action northeast of Verdun on October 14, 1918, MacArthur voluntarily and with distinguished self-sacrifice left his sickbed to lead the attack of his brigade on Hill 288 and 242 and the Cote de Châttillon, the last the key to the entire German line." The recommendation was supported by two lieutenants who gave eyewitness accounts. It was not enough for the War Department and MacArthur was again denied the Medal of Honor, but he did receive a seventh Silver Star.

After the armistice the 42nd Division was ordered into

occupation duty and took over the Ahrweiler district. Most of MacArthur's days were spent greeting distinguished visitors such as the Prince of Wales and trying to keep up the morale of his soldiers, who were anxious to return home. MacArthur headquartered in an elaborate castle in the town of Sinzig, but it was far from enjoyable. Normally healthy, he became seriously ill twice during this time. First, he developed a throat infection from inhaling too much gas, probably from not wearing a mask at the front. Then he had a bout with diphtheria that kept him bedridden.

On March 16, 1919, Pershing reviewed the Rainbow near Remagen where he pinned the Distinguished Service Medal on MacArthur, who wore a steel helmet for the occasion. In April 1919, the division entrained for Brest and Saint-Nazaire where they boarded ships and returned to the United States. MacArthur traveled in luxury aboard the converted German ocean liner *Leviathan*, occupying a five-thousand-dollar suite that consisted of four rooms and three baths. "It filled me with excitement to change my bed and bath each evening," he said.[6]

The division reached New York on April 25, 1919, to little fanfare. MacArthur was the first to disembark, wearing a full-length raccoon coat and a new scarf knitted by his mother. There were no screaming crowds or a welcome parade. It must have reminded MacArthur of his father when he returned from the Philippines and was snubbed at the San Francisco dock. He wrote to a former aide that it was a "sad, gloomy, end of the Rainbow." New York City did throw a ball that evening in his honor at the Waldorf Astoria and MacArthur showed up decked out in full uniform for the first time in months.

MacArthur rests
comfortably
in a chair left
behind by the
original lord
of St. Benoit
Chateau, France
(1918).

MacArthur
relaxing at
the St. Benoit
Chateau,
France (1918).

MacArthur and a group of U.S. Army and Philippine officers wade ashore at Leyte Island, Philippines Islands (1944).

MacArthur wearing his trademark field martial's cap and clenching a corn cob pipe (1944).

SEVEN

West Point

MACARTHUR RETURNED HOME from France the most decorated officer in the American army, but such celebrity didn't guarantee a real future in a military that slimmed down for peacetime duty. America was proud of its war heroes but yearned for a return to normalcy and isolation from the world's problems. MacArthur and other combatants saw things differently. The so-called "war to end all wars" was likely a precursor to even deadlier conflicts looming on the horizon and they needed to ready the military for what was ahead.

Almost immediately after the *Leviathan* docked in New York MacArthur was ordered to Washington for a meeting with Chief of Staff Peyton March. He was well aware of MacArthur's leadership ability on the battlefield and assumed this could be transferred into academia. March told MacArthur that his next assignment was superintendent of West Point and it would commence in June.

MacArthur was dumbfounded and told March, "I am not an educator, I am a field soldier." Furthermore, he said, "there are so many of my old professors there, I can't do it." March ignored him and confidently told MacArthur, "Yes . . . you can do it" and who was MacArthur kidding? He adored West Point and the opportunity to return not as an instructor, which was more typical of officers, but as its superintendent was a great honor.

At thirty-nine MacArthur became the youngest superintendent at West Point since Sylvanus Thayer held the position immediately after the War of 1812. Regardless of his age the task of leading West Point was going to be a difficult challenge. March warned MacArthur that the United States Military Academy was "forty years behind the times . . . and in a state of disorder and confusion." The chief of staff made it clear: "Revitalize and revamp the Academy."[1]

In reality it didn't take much convincing on March's part. The assignment of superintendent was a coveted one and MacArthur took it on with gusto. Before leaving for New York he was temporarily assigned to the General Staff and used that time wisely. MacArthur reacquainted himself with West Point's academic curriculum, which hadn't changed much since his graduation sixteen years before. He met informally with other officers who knew West Point's current state and read reports he found among the files kept by the War Department. MacArthur now had an idea of what March was talking about.

The United States Military Academy was stale and he was anxious to implement a number of recommendations that he hoped would modernize the school. Congress was going to be his biggest obstacle. They "threatened to strip the school to a skeleton," he learned. MacArthur feared that soon his country's political leaders would close down West Point and place a larger focus on reserve officer training programs at civilian colleges.

MacArthur returned to West Point on June 12, 1919, with no fanfare. It was just like 1899 all over again. Pinky, who was then sixty-seven years old and in poor health, accompanied her son and they moved into the superintendent's house together. Typically a new superintendent was treated to an extravagant change of command ceremony and a review of the Corps of Cadets. But MacArthur chose to begin the task at hand and forego such pomp and circumstance. "They'll see me soon enough," he declared.

His changes were fast and controversial. He recognized the immediacy in implementing the changes since the typical post of superintendent was about four years in length. He first needed to adjust the attitude at the academy. The instructors were his first target and this not only included the educators who taught history, math, science, and other core courses, but also the officers who specialized in leadership.

The education at West Point, he correctly perceived, was out of date. MacArthur said the instructors "have become set and smug. They deliver the same schedule year after year with the blessed unction that they have reached the zenith of education."[2] And as far as battlefield leadership was concerned, that, too, was antiquated. His experience on the Western Front had taught him that warfare had become much more complex and future warriors needed to be prepared for an evolving war. He sarcastically queried: "How long are we going to prepare for the War of 1812?" The new breed of officers, MacArthur said, need to improvise and "such changed conditions will require a modification in type of the officer, a type possessing all of the cardinal military virtues of yore, but possessing an intimate understanding of his fellows, a comprehensive grasp of world and national affairs."[3]

MacArthur envisioned that a future army officer would inspire others through confidence and personal actions, just as he had done with the doughboys of the Rainbow Division during the fall and summer of 1918. Through various reforms MacArthur envisioned officers who developed "initiative and force of character." First and foremost he wanted more involvement between tactical officers and cadets. In the past the cadets considered tactical officers to be ogres whose sole purpose was to inflict fear and discipline. Now, tactical officers would in a sense act as company commanders and teach the inexperienced cadets how to deal with issues and discipline at the unit level. To enhance the atmosphere of mentoring, MacArthur ordered them to move into the barracks with their cadets. This proved successful. The bond between the two augmented professionalism within the Corps of Cadets.

A more controversial reform was the transfer of summer training from Fort Clinton to the regular army post at Fort Dix, New Jersey. Fort Clinton was located on the academy grounds and the cadets spent the morning parading and drilling, while the afternoons were more leisurely. In the evening cadets typically dined in a large tent, enjoying extravagant meals served to them by sharply dressed waiters. To someone like MacArthur who recently had spent almost two years eating army rations, such summer activities were "a ludicrous caricature of life in the field." Now under his watch cadets were trained during the summer by regular army noncommissioned officers and soldiers in the use of modern weaponry and took part in realistic field exercises. He explained his rationale in some detail:

> Consciously and unconsciously during their stay in the same cantonment with the enlisted men of the Regular Army, they absorb a vast amount of useful knowledge of the soldiers whom they will later command. They gain in those qualities of self-confidence and assurance which are so valuable to efficient leadership. They learn more of human nature; they acquire understanding, sympathy, and tact. The entire experience both broadens and deepens their character.[4]

Not surprisingly MacArthur wanted the cadets to become more involved in athletics. There was no doubt in his mind that physical fitness contributed greatly to battlefield performance. "It was apparent from the experiences of the World War," he wrote, "that a course of training should be planned not only to fit future officers physically for the rigors of military service, but also to qualify them as physical directors and instructors for their future commands . . . additionally, the war had shown the value of organized group athletics in creating and maintaining morale."[5]

When he had attended West Point, cadets were forbidden to leave unless given special permission. MacArthur had always hated that rule and now that he was in charge, cadets were encouraged to vacate the grounds of the academy for six hours and they received a stipend of five dollars a month to spend however they saw fit. A first class club was established so plebes could have greater interaction with officers. He felt a cadet's lack of social interaction could be corrected "by allowing certain privileges common to all higher institutions of learning. This would serve both as a relaxation from the rigid grind of study and training, and as a means of keeping in touch with life outside the walls of the institution. They were no longer to be walled up within the Academy limits, but were to be treated as responsible young men."[6]

More significantly MacArthur wanted the cadets to have a greater knowledge of world affairs and he directed that each cadet receive two newspapers daily. Furthermore, cadets taking the economics and government course were required to discuss current events at the beginning of each class. Cadets were also allowed to start their own newspaper, the *Bray*. All of this was based on his experience during World War I and his belief that future officers should not only be well versed in the military, but should equally understand political, economic, and social conditions around the world.

Among MacArthur's more influential reforms was the Cadet Honor Code, which had its roots in a system developed by Sylvanus Thayer. It implied a cadet's word was always accepted and thus he was expected to always tell the truth. MacArthur expanded upon this by organizing a thirteen-member honor committee comprised of first classmen who represented each company in the Corps of Cadets.

MacArthur frequently left West Point for Washington to testify before military affairs and appropriations committees. It often was a frustrating task as he tried in vain to argue the army's case for increased troop strength and more funds to keep it functioning at an acceptable level. But this was to no avail. He could only watch as Congress slashed and cut the army's budget. Congress even rejected his pleas to increase the size of the Corps of Cadets and expand West Point's plant and facilities. Congress passed the National Defense Act in 1920 that established the regular force at 288,000 enlisted men and eventually 18,000 officers.

MacArthur did win one battle with Congress. In the spring of 1920 they reestablished the four-year program at West Point. It had been shortened to three years when the United States entered World War I so that officers could be placed in the field at a faster rate. One of MacArthur's biographers called him the "Father of the New West Point."[7] His accomplishments during a limited time were startling. Yet, not everyone was on board with his reforms.

Halfway into his third year as superintendent, MacArthur received the disappointing news that he was to be removed. Normally a superintendent's assignment was four years, but on November 22, 1921, General Pershing, now chief of staff, informed MacArthur that he was being assigned overseas duty at the end of the academic year. Pershing said it was the "decision of the War Department to make the regulation with reference to Foreign Service applicable to the entire official personnel of the Army. The roster shows you to be high up for this service."[8] MacArthur learned later he was heading to the Philippines.

Rumors flew as to the reason for MacArthur's early departure. Was it his clashing with Congress over funding for the U.S. Military Academy or the abruptness of his reforms that forced Pershing to take action? Either was quite possible. Irate members of Congress may have told Pershing and Secretary of War John Weeks to remove MacArthur. More likely it was Pershing and Weeks who tired of him. But an even uglier rumor was floating around the halls of the War Department.

Just two weeks before heading to the Philippines, MacArthur announced his engagement to Mrs. Louise Cromwell Brooks, a wealthy Philadelphia widow. Her father was Oliver E. Cromwell, a well-to-do New York lawyer and yachtsman and her stepfather was Edward T. Stotesbury, a Philadelphia banker whose estimated wealth was well over a hundred million dollars. Before she met MacArthur, Louise had married into money. Her former husband, Walter J. Brooks, was a Baltimore socialite who earned his riches in contracting. They had two children, a son and daughter. MacArthur and Brooks met in September 1921 when Louise came up to West Point with some army officers she knew. MacArthur became infatuated with her immediately and she reciprocated his affection. With his busy schedule they did not see much of each other, but MacArthur sent Louise a steady stream of correspondence.

News of MacArthur's impending marriage set the rumor mill in motion again—and for good reason. Prior to meeting Douglas, Louise had been linked to Pershing. During the war she and Walter had lived in Paris and it's possible her social status and good looks drew Pershing toward her, although his biographers have found no evidence to verify they were romantically involved. They continued their friendship after both returned to the United States and Louise served as his hostess on various occasions. But when her marriage began falling apart in 1919, it was Pershing's aide, Colonel John G. (Harry) Quekemeyer, who pursued Louise. Supposedly a week before accepting MacArthur's marriage proposal she had agreed to marry Quekemeyer. Apparently there was no truth to the stories floating around the halls of the War Department that Pershing removed MacArthur from West Point out of spite.[9]

At the end of January 1922, Pershing announced that MacArthur's replacement as superintendent would be Brigadier General Fred W. Sladen. An 1890 graduate of West Point, Sladen had returned as a tactical instructor and company commander when MacArthur was a cadet. MacArthur, obviously still miffed about being replaced, predicted to his West Point adjutant, Major William A. Ganoe, that Sladen would reverse many of his reforms. This proved to be correct and perhaps that is the reason Pershing selected him.

Before he left West Point, MacArthur received a letter from Pershing that detailed a *faux pas* the soon-to-be-former superintendent had committed. MacArthur had recently testified before Congress and Pershing wanted to know why he had not called on the Secretary of War or Pershing when he was in Washington. It seemed that Weeks had wanted to discuss matters relating to West Point with MacArthur and felt snubbed by him. Pershing was told to find out why.

MacArthur responded at once to Pershing's rebuke with a

reasonable excuse. He was ordered by the adjutant general to report before Congress in less than twenty-four hours and had little time to prepare for the trip. He also told Pershing that "it has never been customary for the Superintendent to report for immediate instructions to his military superiors when summoned by a committee of Congress." Furthermore, he informed Pershing, "In this particular case it would have been practically impossible to have reported for such consultation even if I had known it was desired, on account of short notice given by the War Department order."

MacArthur then took the high road by apologizing. He told Pershing: "I regret exceedingly if this incident may have given any impression of discourtesy to two superior officers whom I hold in the highest respect and esteem."[10] The matter was then apparently forgotten and MacArthur prepared for his next assignment and life as a newly married man, at least for a little while.

Douglas and Louise married on Valentine's Day 1922 at Louise's mother's seafront mansion in Palm Beach, Florida. The other love of MacArthur's life, Pinky, was not in attendance. She was too weak after suffering a heart attack in late November 1921. MacArthur and Louise moved out of the superintendent's quarters in late June 1922, took Pinky to Washington so she could live with Arthur's family, and enjoyed two months of leave before traveling to the Philippines.[11]

Finding His Way in the Army

AFTER A MONTH at sea on board the *Logan*, the MacArthurs arrived at the Manila dock in early October 1922. As the highest ranking officer on the ship, MacArthur's baggage went in the hold first and somehow Douglas, Louise, and her two children managed to fill it with several trunks, hat boxes, and suitcases; so full that each of the other passengers could only bring one trunk. This was in addition to several cars brought by the MacArthurs that took up enough space to prevent anyone else from loading a vehicle.

MacArthur took over the peaceful command of the Military District of Manila. It had been almost two decades since he had been there and at that time the Americans and Filipinos were embroiled in a deadly guerilla war. But that was long over and the country was

well pacified. The former insurgents were now farmers and labor-
ers. No longer was there animosity toward Americans. With little
to do MacArthur developed relationships with Filipino leaders,
most prominently Manuel Quezon. He led the ruling Nacionalista
party, whose goal was to obtain Philippine independence.

Also in the Philippines with MacArthur was Leonard Wood,
who held the post of governor general. The two often discussed defending the Philippines against a potential attack by
the Japanese. It was a hot topic in Washington and shortly after
MacArthur arrived in Manila, the Joint Army and Navy Board
drafted War Plan Orange. Planning for war with various countries
was one of the more important functions the board was charged
with and they named each plan with a different color. Black was
for Germany, red was for Great Britain, and orange was for Japan.

In the event the United States went to war with Japan—and
many in the War and Navy Departments were convinced it would
happen—the Philippines would play a vital role. In such case the
Philippines Department held responsibility for Corregidor and
Bataan, located at the mouth of Manila Harbor. In theory this pre-
vented the Japanese from entering the harbor. Just how this would
occur when Congress was limiting funds to the Philippines, thus
preventing an increase in troops and matériel, was anyone's guess.
Certain members of Congress believed the United States had no
business holding on to the Philippines and a bill was introduced
in 1924 calling for the military and civilian forces to withdraw in
twenty years.

As commander of the Manila District, MacArthur had the
31st Infantry Regiment under him and he enjoyed spending

time with his soldiers. Just as he was becoming comfortable, MacArthur and his family rushed back to Washington because Pinky's health had taken a turn for the worse. Her heart was weak and if it hadn't been for the miraculous work of army physician Dr. Howard J. Hutter, she might have died. Hutter later became MacArthur's physician and close friend. MacArthur's brother Arthur also rushed to his mother's side. This was the last time Douglas saw him. In December 1923, Arthur died suddenly of appendicitis. While in Washington, MacArthur visited with Secretary of War Weeks to ask if there was possibly another assignment that would bring him stateside. Neither he nor Louise was excited about Manila, but Weeks had nothing to offer and told MacArthur to be patient.

Upon his return to the Philippines in June 1923, MacArthur was given command of the 23rd Brigade of the Philippines Division. MacArthur was also placed in charge of mapping and surveying the Bataan Peninsula. He took over command of the troubled Philippines Division when a mutiny broke out among the ranks of Filipino scouts. They were protesting the fact that their pay allowances and benefits did not equal the pay and benefits of the American soldiers in the division. There was little MacArthur could do to resolve the issue since funding in the Philippines was limited and there was racial prejudice within the War Department toward the Filipino soldiers. Meanwhile MacArthur continued to seek out another assignment and inquired about posts as military attaché in London and Tokyo but was rejected in both instances.

Thanks once again to his mother, MacArthur received another star. Pinky, obviously on the mend from her latest bout with heart problems, wrote another long letter to Pershing requesting that he promote her son to major general. Rumors were circulating throughout Washington that Pershing was about to step down as chief of staff and Pinky unabashedly asked him: "Won't you be real good and sweet—The 'Dear Old Jack' of long ago—and give me some assurance that you will give my Boy his well earned promotion before you leave the Army?" Pinky's influence seems to have worked since ten days after Pershing handed over the position of chief of staff to Major General John L. Hines, MacArthur was promoted to major general. He also got his wish to leave the Philippines and in the spring of 1925 he returned to the United States to command the IV Corps area based in Atlanta, Georgia.

It was a lively position that included helping the governor of North Carolina rescue trapped miners in the western region of that state. In the summer MacArthur organized the training of young men of the Reserve Officers Training Corps (ROTC), the Organized Reserve Corps (ORC), and the Citizen Military Training Camps (CMTC), who poured into the various forts and camps under MacArthur's responsibility. This assignment was short-lived as MacArthur was sent to command the III Corps area, which encompassed the Washington-Chesapeake Bay region. The family moved into Rainbow Hill, an estate at Eccleston, Maryland, owned by Louise. Only two months into his new command, MacArthur was detailed to serve as a judge in the court-martial of Brigadier General Billy Mitchell.

The trial became the most celebrated news story of 1925. Mitchell was accused of violating the 96th Article of War, but there were eight specifications to the charge that in essence said his conduct brought disservice to the military. He had been an out-spoken critic of the War and Navy Department's lack of support for aviation. Since World War I, during which Mitchell showed the potential for air power on the battlefield, he had been on a crusade through speeches, articles, and books to promote air power. But it was his public statements through the press that did Mitchell in.

After thunderstorms over Ohio downed the navy's rigid airship the USS *Shenandoah* in 1925, Mitchell blamed the navy's handling of the dirigible, accusing the sea service, the War Department, and by inference President Calvin Coolidge's administration of criminal negligence. Coolidge fired back and ordered his secretary of war, Dwight Davis, to get rid of him. MacArthur was the youngest of thirteen judges and none of them had any experience with the air service. MacArthur called his detail "one of the most distasteful orders I ever received."[1]

MacArthur did not say a word throughout the seven-week trial, probably because of the great affection he had for Mitchell and it is also likely he didn't want to rock the boat and affect his own career. They had last seen each other in January 1924 when Mitchell, as assistant chief of air service, visited the Philippines to inspect the virtually nonexistent air defenses on the island. Found guilty as charged, Mitchell was ordered stripped of his duties for five years, with his pay eventually cut in half. Two months later he resigned from the army. Although the individual votes were not made public, MacArthur claimed that he voted for acquittal.[2]

The next few years were depressing times to be in the military. Congress slashed the army's budget, which was reflected in the nation's antiquated fortifications. It was particularly true of the harbor and coastal defenses that were part of III Corps area, despite the fact they were the first line of defense in keeping the nation's capital safe from invasion. He continued to promote the CMTC summer programs, but they had limited success because it was not economically feasible for parents to allow their sons to attend camp when they were needed on the farm during the summer. Also hindering the camps was an antiwar pacifism that prevailed over the country. This troubled MacArthur deeply. He often spoke about the implications of unpreparedness and how it only encouraged aggressors and ultimately led to costly wars.

During one of his more celebrated speeches, MacArthur addressed a crowd of distinguished civilian and military leaders at a banquet in the spring of 1927 that was organized by the Soldiers and Sailors Club to commemorate America's entry into the First World War. He outlined the various conflicts raging throughout the world and predicted that

> it does not seem unlikely that our streets will again be filled with marching men and our country again have need of our services . . . The provisions of our national defense act should be fully carried out. Total disarmament is unthinkable. No one takes seriously the equally illogical plan of disbanding our fire departments to stop fires or disbanding our police departments to stop crime.[3]

He then told the sympathetic audience that it was the citizen soldier who would become the backbone of America's national defense. MacArthur ended the speech on an uplifting note: "And when the bloody test comes, some American chief, on the day of victory, is going to thank God for what this nation is now building up in its citizen soldiers."[4]

If it wasn't enough to stand by and watch his beloved army disintegrate before his eyes, MacArthur faced the same troubles at home with his marriage. Their lifestyles simply did not match. Louise was especially unhappy when they lived in the Philippines because she and her husband did not share the same social interests. MacArthur preferred to spend his free time, which was rare, with Quezon and other Filipinos whom he considered friends. He also enjoyed the company of his stepchildren, especially Walter, who MacArthur taught how to ride.

Louise countered by becoming more involved in social events held by the elite in Manila. She also repeatedly encouraged MacArthur to leave the army and try his hand at a civilian job. Louise even helped arrange a position for him with J. P. Morgan and Company, but he was not interested. The marriage seemed to improve slightly when they moved to Rainbow Hill. Louise could resume her social life, and she even managed to get MacArthur to join the elite Green Spring Valley Club, where the wealthy took part in foxhunting, among other endeavors.

All of this was fleeting and by August 1927 the MacArthurs were separated. Louise moved to New York City and took up residence at the Beverly on 50th Street, while her husband remained at Rainbow Hill. The marriage ended in divorce in 1929; MacArthur was back in Manila at this time. Because of their prominence, MacArthur as a general and his wife a socialite, the news media took an interest in the breakup. Louise told reporters that "General MacArthur and I divorced because we were wholly incompatible to each other. I have the greatest respect and admiration for him and we part friends."[5] Louise married and divorced two more times. She died of a heart attack at age seventy-five in Washington.

Typical of MacArthur, he did not discuss his personal problems in public and he only slightly mentioned this episode in *Reminiscences*: "In February 1922 I entered into matrimony, but it was not successful, and ended in divorce years later for mutual incompatibility."[6]

Certainly hurt by the failure of his marriage and missing the company of his stepchildren, MacArthur focused on his work. Then a once-in-a-lifetime opportunity presented itself in the fall of 1927. The president of the American Olympic Committee died suddenly and with the next Olympics only ten months away, a replacement was needed immediately. MacArthur was natural for the position and this brought him back to life. He was a strong advocate of athletics and had the leadership ability to take over the post. MacArthur's old acquaintance, Charles P. Summerall, was now army chief of staff and gave him permission to take the position, believing it would be good publicity for the service.

Although he remained commander of III Corps, most of his time was spent on Olympic business. During the summer of 1928, he accompanied the American team to Amsterdam for the Ninth Olympiad. His presidency did not go without a hitch. In one instance the American sprint champion, Charley Paddock, was accused of accepting money, thus making him ineligible to run in the Olympics since he could no longer be considered an amateur. But MacArthur insisted on taking him to Holland any-way. And when the boxing team coach attempted to withdraw his fighters from competition over protest about a bad decision, MacArthur ordered them to continue fighting their remaining bouts since Americans do not quit. He reveled in the pomp and circumstance of the Olympics and proved to be a great motivator and leader.

> "I rode them all hard along the line," he recounted. "Athletes are among the most temperamental of all persons, but I stormed and pleaded and cajoled. I told them we represented the greatest nation in the world . . . that we had not come 3,000 miles just to lose gracefully that we were there to win, and win decisively."[7]

By the time the games closed, the American team set seven world records, seventeen Olympic records, and earned twice as many medals as any other country. A proud MacArthur gave every team member a gold charm as a token of his appreciation for their good showing. Shortly after returning home from Amsterdam, MacArthur was sent back to Manila and placed in command of the Philippines Department. This time he was thrilled to be there. "No assignment could have pleased me more," he wrote in his memoirs. "I found Manila as bright and lively as ever."[8]

He spent most of his days meeting with Quezon, who "was now the undisputed leader of the Filipinos."[9] Japan was the prime topic of conversation along with how to prepare the island for invasion despite the fact that the troops there were "pitifully inadequate, and Washington apparently had no clear-cut idea with reference to Philippine defense."[10] Henry L. Stimson was the governor general of the island. He and MacArthur formed a strong friendship and according to MacArthur, "He [Stimson] was a preparedness man, and supported my military training program with understanding and vigor."[11] But what was really on MacArthur's mind was the position of chief of staff. A new president was in the White House—Herbert Hoover—who knew about MacArthur's abilities.

In July 1929 MacArthur was offered the position of chief of engineers by Hoover, but he turned it down. He said his official reason was that the chief should be an officer of "outstanding engineering ability and that ability must be of such general recognition as to give him the complete confidence of the engineering profession at large. I had neither of these qualifications."[12] MacArthur didn't really want the job because he thought it would block any chance of becoming chief of staff.

Finally, on August 6, 1930, MacArthur's patience paid off and he fulfilled a long-time dream. Hoover appointed him chief of staff, the youngest officer to ever hold the position. MacArthur claims in his memoirs that he hesitated before accepting the position because he "knew the dreadful ordeal that faced the new Chief of Staff and shrank from it. I wished from the bottom of my heart to stay with troops in a field command," but his mother influenced his decision. Pinky, who was still living in Washington, "sensed what was on my mind and cabled me to accept." MacArthur wrote that she tugged at her son's heartstrings by telling him his father "would be ashamed if [he] showed timidity."[13] Before he left the Philippines the Filipino people organized a number of social events in his honor with a final grand banquet at the Manila Hotel. As he returned to the United States that October, MacArthur knew he would see the Philippines again. After all, the Filipino people had embraced him as one of their own.

Boy Scouts from Philippines visit Chief of Staff MacArthur (1935).

Bonus Marcher's shanty town after it was burned by the D.C. Metropolitan Police (1932).

MacArthur, with his aides, First Lieutenant Thomas J. Davis in the center and Major Dwight D. Eisenhower in the background, during the Bonus March (1932).

NINE

Chief of Staff

As CHIEF OF staff, most days were spent advising the secretary of war, Patrick Hurley, about national preparedness—a topic MacArthur was well acquainted with. Convincing Congress was not so easy. He said, "Congress was bored and annoyed by the Army, which kept on croaking that war would come again and sooner, perhaps, than expected."[1] This was a busy time in MacArthur's life and when he wasn't testifying before disinterested lawmakers, there was his mother to tend to as well as an active social life.

With his new title came a new home, Fort Myers Number One Quarters. Pinky also moved into the stately mansion that overlooked the Potomac River. To accommodate her advanced years and poor health, he had an elevator installed and a sun porch constructed. Divorced for almost a year, MacArthur focused his love life on a mistress he secretly kept in Washington—Isabel Rosario Cooper, a Eurasian girl he had met five months before leaving the Philippines. She was the daughter of an oriental woman and a Scottish businessman living in the Philippines. Isabel eventually followed him to Washington where MacArthur rented an apartment for her in the Hotel Chastleton that she shared with a poodle and closets full of exotic clothing.

Somehow MacArthur kept Isabel hidden from gossip-filled Washington, and most of all hidden from Pinky, who would not have tolerated such behavior. Otherwise, MacArthur had a fairly sedate lifestyle. He wore civilian clothes to his office at the State, War and Navy Building, ignored the press, and rode home each day to lunch with his mother. In the evenings he avoided dinner and cocktail parties and preferred to stay home reading books he had acquired from his father's vast library. There was also a flamboyant side to MacArthur that came to light. Outlandish clothing had always been part of his persona, as exhibited on the Western Front; but as chief of staff, MacArthur took it to a new level. Visitors to his office frequently saw him wearing a Japanese ceremonial kimono, cooling off with an oriental fan, and smoking cigarettes from a jeweled holder. And behind his office chair stood a fifteen-foot-tall mirror that gave the impression he was taller than his real height of five feet eleven inches.

As chief of staff, MacArthur also had the occasion to visit Europe. During the first trip in the fall of 1931, he observed French army maneuvers and was presented with the Grand Cross of the Legion Honor by French War Minister Andre Maginot, famous for the defensive line that bears his name. During his second European trip, MacArthur inspected the armies of Turkey, Romania, Hungary, Poland, and Austria. While Europe remained at peace, on the other side of the world hostilities broke out between Japan and China. Eventually the powerful Japanese army captured all of South Manchuria. Then in early 1932 the Japanese attacked Shanghai, and although a large number of Americans resided there, none were harmed. At the urging of MacArthur and Secretary of State Stimson, President Hoover sent the 31st Infantry from the Philippines and a company of Marines to Shanghai, elevating the possibility of war between the United States and Japan. The Japanese backed down and withdrew that May.

As the First World War became a distant memory, Americans were becoming more and more complacent. By the 1930s the pacifist movement in the United States was at its peak, influenced by outspoken clergy. MacArthur was invited to respond to a poll, conducted by leading clergymen and published in *The World Tomorrow*, that showed alarming numbers of ordained clergy in America would not serve as armed combatants in the next war, even as chaplains.

Among other opinions, the chief of staff wrote:

> I can think of no principles more high and holy than those for which our national sacrifices have been made in the past. History teaches us that religion and patriotism have always gone hand in hand, while atheism has invariably been accompanied by radicalism, communism, bolshevism, and other enemies of free government.

He finished the letter with:

> I confidently believe that a red-blooded and virile humanity which loves peace devotedly, but is willing to die in the defense of the right, is Christian from center to circumference, and will continue to be dominant in the future as in the past.[2]

MacArthur firmly believed that Communism was alive and well in America and an incident during the summer of 1932 made him even more concerned about the direction his country was heading. The 1930s were a time of peril in the United States. Millions of Americans were out of work and the country was in the midst of the Great Depression. President Hoover handled the crisis in a modest way with various reforms, but there were no signs of an economic upturn on the horizon.

Among the unemployed were more than three million First World War veterans who were counting on their government to make good on the Adjusted Compensation Act, which Congress had enacted in 1924. Dangling in front of them was a much-needed one-thousand-dollar bonus in the form of a bond that was to mature in 1945 or on the death of the holder. The problem was the Hoover administration did not have the money to pay the bonus and satisfying the needs of the veterans was not a top priority, so they thought.

Various veterans groups around the country vented to the news media and also organized protests, but Hoover ignored them. During the winter of 1931–32, they descended upon Washington. A few lucky ones got work performing kitchen or stable duties at Fort Myer, Virginia, but tens of thousands of other veterans arrived in the nation's capital homeless. While some took up residence in condemned buildings blocks from the White House, the vast majority created a shantytown in the Anacostia section of the city. To mock the president it became known among other names as "Hooverville." Their numbers expanded daily and, as a result, Washington was overcome with paranoia. They were called the "Bonus Army" and it was the belief of many in the Hoover administration that they had been infiltrated by hoards of Communists. In reality they were led by two known Communists and perhaps a few others joined up. But even this paltry number was too many for the White House and the War Department.

MacArthur had no time for Communists or anyone who was antigovernment. At first he thought they were of little threat, but as the Bonus Army grew, MacArthur's patience decreased and he counseled Secretary of War Hurley that the War Department must take action. Meanwhile most of the marchers formed the Bonus Expeditionary Force (BEF) under the leadership of a well-respected combat veteran, Walter F. Williams. Their goal was a peaceful demonstration for an early payment of the bonus, not to create havoc. Yet, this was not to be, although some on Capitol Hill were sympathetic to their plight and one congressman created legislation to not only pay the bonus but also to feed and shelter the BEF. This went nowhere as the House and Senate could not agree on a compromise.

The situation reached a climactic and chaotic conclusion at the end of July. Congress had adjourned a couple of weeks before and the only thing the veterans had gained was authorization to borrow against their certificates for transportation to get back home. Some took the money and left, while about ten thousand stayed in Washington, vowing to remain until 1945 if that is what it took. It appeared the Hoover administration had dodged a bullet. But July 28 was a day Washington would not soon forget.

Until then the District of Columbia police—led by a former army brigadier general and West Point classmate of MacArthur's—had watched over the bonus marchers. Things got out of hand the morning of the twenty-eighth when the police attempted to evict eleven hundred veterans who were squatting in condemned buildings. The squatters resisted and the police sought help from Hoover. As a result, two of the bonus marchers were killed by police. Later that day President Hoover directed Hurley to cooperate with the police to "surround the affected area and clear it without delay."[3] Then Hurley was to help the police lock up all of the bonus marchers and identify their leaders and have them tried in court.

Hurley conferred with MacArthur and the two concluded that it was an impossible order to carry out and should be amended to have the army clear the entire city of marchers, not just those harassing the DC police. Itching to pick a fight, an excited MacArthur declared: "We are going to break the back of the BEF."[4] He ordered the 3rd Cavalry Regiment, stationed nearby at Fort Myer, to Washington for riot duty. Led by its flamboyant executive officer, Major George S. Patton, the regiment arrived on horseback wearing steel helmets and gas masks. The impressive bunch also carried sabers as though they were about to attack hostile Indians on the western frontier.

MacArthur started the day dressed in civilian clothes but insisted upon witnessing the operations firsthand and sent a staff member to retrieve his uniform from home. Major Dwight D. Eisenhower was working as an aide to Assistant Chief of Staff Brigadier General George Van Horn Mosley. MacArthur liked the young officer and wanted him by his side as the army confronted the BEF. Eisenhower, the more levelheaded of the two, felt MacArthur's presence would be provocative and advised the chief of staff to think otherwise. He told his boss, "I thought it had the aspect of a riot rather than a big military movement, and so told him that I thought this was inadvisable, that the chief of staff should not dignify the incident by going out himself."[5]

MacArthur ignored Eisenhower's advice. Fourteen years before he had fought at the front with the Rainbow Division and MacArthur was not about to lead from the rear now. Eisenhower quickly went home, put on his uniform, and joined MacArthur on the streets of DC.

Besides the cavalry, MacArthur also called out the infantry and at 4:00 p.m. the army commanders received the signal to disperse the BEF. It must have been difficult for some of the soldiers to undertake this operation since many of them had likely fought on the same battlefields as the bonus marchers. But they carried out their orders while thousands of spectators lined the streets showering them with bricks and bottles. The soldiers responded by tear-gassing the crowd and then used some tear gas on the bonus marchers as they were driven back to their shantytown in the Anacostia flats.

Growing uneasy about the operation, Hoover sent a new

order forbidding the army from chasing after the marchers across the Anacostia Bridge, or to evict the inhabitants.
MacArthur was not around to receive the orders directly, but
Mosely was and delivered word to his boss. "He was very much
annoyed at having his plans interfered with,"[6] Mosely wrote.
The common perception of Bonus March historians is that
Mosely may have lied and never delivered Hoover's message
to MacArthur.[7] Regardless, Hurley apparently understood the
president's orders clearly and twice informed MacArthur not
to enter Anacostia. Eisenhower's recollections are even more
interesting: "I went up to the General and said, 'There's a man
here who has some orders about this.' He said, 'I don't want
to hear them and I don't want to see them. Get him away.'"
Apparently MacArthur, at least according to Eisenhower, did
not like to be bothered by "people coming down and pretend-
ing to bring him orders." So MacArthur, with some truth, could
say he never received the orders.[8]

In any event MacArthur issued orders at 9:30 for the troops
to cross the bridge and clear out the shantytown. As the soldiers
approached a fire broke out and Hooverville quickly burned
down. The DC police were already there and they eventually
cleared the camp of any remaining inhabitants. MacArthur was
by now back at the War Department and he and Hurley held a
joint news conference. Convinced that the BEF was rife with
Communists, MacArthur bragged that his actions had just saved
the country from "incipient revolution."

Experienced in the ways of public affairs while working for
Secretary of War Baker, MacArthur also told the news-hungry

press: "If President Hoover had not acted when he did he would have been faced with a serious situation. Another week might have meant that the government was in peril. He had reached the end of an extraordinary patience and had gone to the very limit to avoid friction before using force. Had the President not acted when he did he would have been derelict in his duty."[9]

Although there is no television or Internet coverage from that period, plenty of photographs document the events and most are unflattering. One of the more famous shows MacArthur with a cigarette hanging from his mouth and a clearly chagrined Eisenhower standing in the background. It is a startling image and documents how uncomfortable the situation was for all participants.

Publicly MacArthur downplayed the incident, but it obviously affected him for the remainder of his life. In *Reminiscences* he used almost six pages to detail the "poignant episode during my role as Chief of Staff." It was an ugly incident whether one believes it was handled correctly or not. In fairness to MacArthur the press exaggerated events and their coverage did not side with him. He rightly complained that the

> most extravagant distortions of what had occurred were widely circulated. I was violently attacked, even blatantly misrepresented before Congress. Speeches pictured me in full dress uniform astride a fiery white charger, bedecked with medals, waving a bloody saber, and leading a mad cavalry charge against unarmed and innocent citizens.[10]

Accepting full responsibility for what occurred, MacArthur offered to resign, but he stayed on while Hoover did not. Hoover

was ousted from office in 1932 and replaced by the former governor of New York, Franklin Delano Roosevelt.[11]

Controversy continued to follow MacArthur. With the
Bonus March fiasco behind him, there was another battle to
fight. His affair with Isabel came to an abrupt halt in 1934. It
stemmed from a lawsuit he filed against journalist Drew Pearson.
MacArthur, never one to hide his political views, was despised
by the liberal press and by Pearson in particular. He continually
attacked MacArthur in print, saying that the general was disloyal
to President Roosevelt and Secretary of War George H. Dern.
MacArthur unwisely decided to defend himself, which backfired.
He sued Pearson for 1.75 million dollars and Pearson was willing
to settle in court. His star witness was Louise, who had been feeding him all kinds of dirt, but she refused to testify and it looked as
if Pearson would lose.

Then Ross Collins, another nemesis of MacArthur's, stepped
forward. Ross was a former Mississippi congressman who had
quarreled with MacArthur over military spending. Collins
told Pearson about Isabel and he eventually tracked her down.
Scorned by MacArthur, she was willing to show Pearson a collection of letters, postcards, and telegrams that offered proof of their
affair. MacArthur's lawyer was contacted and the general was
willing to settle with Pearson out of court. The suit was dropped
and Isabel disappeared.

TEN

Disillusioned

MACARTHUR HAD LONGED to become the army's chief of staff, but the position soon wore thin and he became disillusioned. Despite his persistent prodding, the army never received the funding he believed it deserved. This was reminiscent of when he was superintendent of West Point and stood by and watched as it was whittled down to a new low in men and matériel. There was little support from the American people because the Bonus March incident had left a terrible scar on a country already questioning the need for a strong military.

With a new president came a new direction for the country and MacArthur had to brace himself for what lay ahead. Roosevelt and MacArthur had crossed paths many times during joint committee meetings of the Navy and War Departments before

America entered World War I. Although political opposites, they were mostly on friendly terms while MacArthur remained chief of staff, although Roosevelt was suspicious of him. Supposedly two months after he received his Democratic party's nomination for president, Roosevelt declared MacArthur the second most dangerous man in America behind Senator Huey Long of Louisiana. Militarily the new president was a navy man with a lesser interest in the Army Air Corps. MacArthur, on the other hand, was no fan of the New Deal programs the president authorized to help bring the country out of the depression.

One particular program that excited Roosevelt was the Civilian Conservation Corps (CCC), which was run jointly by the Interior and War Departments. It was Roosevelt's dream to place unemployed young men in camps here they would undertake projects in reforestation, flood control, soil rehabilitation, and the development of National Park facilities. The army's part was to enroll the recruits, put them through a two-week conditioning course, and transport them to work camps to be placed under the direction of the U.S. Forest Service. MacArthur rebuffed the idea since he didn't want the army engaged in relief work, but he cooperated anyway and put the General Staff to work figuring the costs of organizing, supplying, and transporting the units of unemployed men. Eventually MacArthur warmed to the program and looked at the CCC as a valuable training experience for the army and also as a way to promote his officer corps to the public.

The chief of staff and the president continued to be at odds over how the country should prepare for the next war.

The relationship reached a new low when MacArthur and Dern personally appealed to the president about the perils of cutting the national defense budget during a time when Nazi Germany was on the rise and Japan was displaying aggression. They met at the White House and the conversation became heated. MacArthur later admitted that he "spoke recklessly," and told the commander-in-chief something like, "When we lose the next war, and an American boy, lying in the mud with an enemy bayonet through his belly and an enemy foot on his dying throat, spat out his last course, I wanted the name not to be MacArthur, but Roosevelt."[1]

An incensed Roosevelt replied: "You must not talk that way to the President." MacArthur recognized that he had crossed the line and offered to resign. But Roosevelt calmed down and told him, "Don't be foolish, Douglas, you and the budget must get together on this."[2] Prone to fits of nausea when he was stressed or nervous, MacArthur vomited on the White House steps after the meeting.

Even though the tenure of chief of staff was usually capped at four years, much to MacArthur's surprise, Roosevelt kept him on for another year. But he was virtually powerless in battling Congress and the president over funding for the army. It was an uphill battle since Roosevelt earmarked most of the country's expenditures for his New Deal programs. From time to time Roosevelt invited MacArthur to the White House for informal conversations that had little to do with military affairs, but rather to sound him out on impending legislation. Roosevelt told MacArthur, "To me, you are the symbol of the conscience of the American people."[3]

Then to no one's surprise, in December 1934 Roosevelt announced he was replacing his chief of staff as soon as he could find a new one. But for the time being he would be kept on "in order to obtain the benefit of General MacArthur's experience in handling War Department legislation in the coming session."[4] Thanks to Manuel Quezon, who was inaugurated as the first president of the Philippines, MacArthur remained employed.

Faced with the daunting task of leading his country toward independence while Japan lurked in the background, Quezon visited the United States and met with MacArthur to ask his opinion on how the Philippines could be defended after it became self-sufficient. They discussed the costs involved and how to build up a regular army supplemented by a larger reserve force. Then Quezon asked MacArthur a pointed question: "General, do you think that the Philippines, once independent, can defend itself?" MacArthur responded immediately, "I don't think that the Philippines can defend themselves, I know they can." Furthermore MacArthur said: "We cannot just turn around and leave you alone. All these many years we have helped you in education, sanitation, road-building, and even in the practice of self-government, but we have done nothing in the way of preparing you to defend yourselves against a foreign foe."[5]

Before returning home Quezon asked MacArthur to come to the Philippines to commence building up the island nation's defenses. At first he hesitated accepting, in hopes that Roosevelt would have a better offer. The president did just that. On March 4, 1935, Roosevelt appointed MacArthur military advisor to the Philippine Commission. His assignment was straightforward:

prepare the island nation's defense for independence in 1946. Because they were still an American colony, MacArthur was basically on loan from the army. This was an ideal arrangement. MacArthur could return to the country he loved, still be directly involved with war planning, and draw two salaries.

Roosevelt approved MacArthur going to the Philippines for basically two reasons. First, he did not want him around as a potential presidential candidate in 1936. And second, it was Roosevelt's way of telling the Japanese to not be so hasty about taking the Philippines because I have MacArthur there to prepare for the defenses. Regarding the upcoming presidential election there is no evidence to suggest that MacArthur seriously considered throwing his hat into the ring even though he was highly thought of in the Republican Party and by conservative Americans; no doubt would have been a worthy challenger.

Before MacArthur departed for Manila, he insisted that Major Dwight D. Eisenhower join him as chief of staff. The relationship between the two has been described as enigmatic. Eisenhower was at various times secretary, adviser, staff officer, and as one of his biographers wrote, "frequently, whipping boy." Eisenhower earned a reputation within the General Staff as hardworking and loyal, just the kind of man MacArthur needed by his side. Eisenhower explained to a biographer why he was attracted to MacArthur: "He did have a hell of an intellect! My God, but he was smart. He had a *brain*."[6]

Although they knew each other before, their working relationship began in January 1933 when Eisenhower moved into a tiny alcove no larger than a broom closet behind a slatted door adjacent to MacArthur's large inner sanctum. MacArthur's method of summoning Eisenhower to his presence was to simply shout. Eisenhower wrote that MacArthur "spoke and wrote in purple splendor." Most of their discussions turned to monologues in which MacArthur pontificated and Eisenhower listened, often mystified by his chief's references to himself in the third person, such as telling his aide: "So MacArthur went over to the Senator, and said, Senator . . ."[7] Eisenhower eventually became immune to such odd behavior.

At various times other staff officers also observed MacArthur's eccentricities. Major General Lewis H. Brereton, who took command of the air forces in the Philippines right before World War II, noted that MacArthur was extremely well dressed and rarely perspired in the tropical heat. "I have never seen him looking otherwise than as if he had just put on a fresh uniform."[8] Supposedly MacArthur had a full wardroom complete with twenty-three uniforms and suits, the latter custom made by a Chinese tailor. He changed clothes three times a day: for breakfast, lunch, and dinner.

Sidney L. Huff, MacArthur's naval adviser, often watched in amusement as his boss would light a cigarette, then "immediately put it down on his desk and start walking back and forth across the room." Other times Huff saw MacArthur stop at his desk and "line up a dozen pencils that were already in a neat pattern or turn them around and push the points carefully into line. But always he went back to pacing and thinking out loud"[9]—he could not talk sitting down.

When in Washington MacArthur was chauffeured to Capitol

Hill and around the city by limousine, while Eisenhower, whose business frequently required him to visit the same places, took a streetcar or taxi. According to Eisenhower, MacArthur did not ever offer him a ride in or the use of his car. This selfishness on MacArthur's part bothered Eisenhower the remainder of his life. "No matter what happens later you never forget something like that," he confessed to a reporter shortly before his death. Eisenhower seemed equally awed and angered by MacArthur.

Although impressed by his intelligence, his charm, and his flattery toward a junior officer, Eisenhower deplored MacArthur's posturing and unwillingness to accept advice, as exhibited during the summer of 1932. Overall, their relationship can be viewed as positive. Eisenhower was on the fence about joining his boss in Manila and finally decided to go when MacArthur allowed him to nominate another officer to accompany them and share in the duties. Eisenhower chose an old friend and West Point classmate, Major James Basevi Ord.

In October, MacArthur, Pinky, her daughter-in-law Mary (Arthur's widow), their personal physician Dr. Hutter, Ord, and his family and various staff left San Francisco aboard the *President Hoover*. Pinky was now eighty-four and very ill. She spent the voyage confined to her cabin, carefully watched over by Mary and Dr. Hutter. Her son, on the other hand, busied himself with another passenger, Jean Marie Faircloth, a charming Southern girl from Murfreesboro, Tennessee. Like Pinky, she had family who fought for the Confederacy during the Civil War. Her grandfather, Captain Richard Beard, opposed Douglas's father at Missionary Ridge.

MacArthur took an immediate liking to Jean, and why not? She was five foot two, one hundred pounds, thirty-seven, and had never been married. The two met during a ship party in honor of Mayor James Curley of Boston. Five years before Jean had inherited a large sum of money and was on her way to Shanghai, then off on a world cruise. Neither plan materialized. She remained in Manila as MacArthur's girlfriend.

MacArthur and Pinky lived in the Manila Hotel where he occupied the six-room, air-conditioned penthouse suite with a large formal drawing room, a library paneled with Philippine mahogany, and two balconies that overlooked the city. One of them opened off the dining room and presented a spectacular view of Bataan and Corregidor. Pinky, unfortunately, never enjoyed the luxurious accommodations. By the time the party reached the Philippines she was dying from cerebral thrombosis. MacArthur made her as comfortable as possible in her own suite adjacent to his. She held out for another month before lapsing into a coma, then passed away a short time later. Pinky's body was kept on dry ice and temporarily interred in Manila with the intention of reburying her in Arlington Cemetery with her husband the next opportunity MacArthur had to return to the States. He mourned her passing heavily and ordered her suite locked and unoccupied for a year. Eisenhower noted that Pinky's death "affected the General's spirit for many months."[10] Eisenhower also lived at the Manila Hotel, but his housing was much smaller than his boss's and had no air-conditioning. The Ords and their two children had taken a house in the city.

MacArthur's mission was to create and train a Philippine

defense force to safeguard a virtually indefensible island nation. By 1936, the urgency increased with each new act of Japanese aggression in Southeast Asia. Hardly anyone in Washington, however, cared about the Philippines, which was seen not only as extremely hard to defend but also of no strategic importance. Eisenhower was already well versed in Philippine problems from his service under MacArthur in Washington. It became virtually impossible to persuade Washington, however, to increase the miniscule Philippine budget. Although MacArthur never accepted the premise, it was soon evident to Eisenhower that "though we worked doggedly through 1936 and 1937, ours was a hopeless venture in a sense. The Philippine government simply could not afford to build a real security from attack."[11]

On his return to the Philippines, MacArthur found there was much work to be done. He was about to introduce a radical program to enhance national defense. His National Defense Act stated that all Filipino boys were required by law to take part in "preparatory military training" from ages ten through seventeen. The training would take place in the public schools and afterward they would advance to the "junior reserve." Then on their twentieth birthday they had to register for five and a half months of active duty in the Philippine army. Girls were not exempt. They were trained in auxiliary service when in public school. MacArthur also wanted the military units spread throughout the various provinces and islands that encompassed the Philippines.

One of MacArthur's conditions for taking the job was that Quezon promote him to the rank of field marshal in the Philippine army. This contradicted American military tradition and appalled

Eisenhower. MacArthur thought that such an exalted rank was necessary to enhance the prestige of his position. He not only accepted the title, but an annual salary of $18,000 plus $15,000 in expenses.[12]

MacArthur was formally appointed as field marshal on August 24, 1936, during an elaborate ceremony at Malacanan Palace. After Quezon read the commission, his wife presented MacArthur with a gold baton. MacArthur was dressed in a specially designed sharkskin uniform adorned with braid, stars, and fancy lapel designs. After the presentation the new field marshal addressed the crowd with a steady reminder of the importance of national defense. For the time being MacArthur was the toast of Manila.

When Quezon formally presented MacArthur with a gold baton as a symbol of his new position, Eisenhower almost choked in disgust, calling the ceremony "rather fantastic." He thought it "pompous and rather ridiculous" for MacArthur "to be the field marshal of a virtually non-existing army. You have been a four-star general," he told him. "This is a proud thing. . . . Why . . . do you want a banana country giving you a field-marshal-ship?"[13] MacArthur not only ignored him, recalled Eisenhower, but also gave him a hard time.

ELEVEN

Domestic Bliss

AFTER A TRYING year in which MacArthur and his staff worked hard to iron out the kinks in the training program for Filipino conscripts, it finally got off the ground in early January 1937. Quezon felt comfortable enough to leave the Philippines and embark on a trip to Washington to confer with the newly appointed high commissioner Paul V. McNutt, former Indiana governor, and with President Roosevelt about gaining Philippines independence at the end of 1938. It was an exhausting trip that included stops in Mexico, Japan, and Europe. Included in the entourage were MacArthur, his aide Captain Thomas J. Davis, and Dr. Hutter.

The trip was mostly a failure. Roosevelt at first refused to meet with Quezon but reluctantly did so after MacArthur intervened.

Roosevelt rejected early independence and Quezon moved on to Capitol Hill where the congressmen who made up the Joint Preparatory Committee on Philippine Affairs sympathized with him. They would not, however, commit to releasing the islands from American control before 1946.

While Quezon made his rounds MacArthur did the same with various War and Navy Department heads in hopes of obtaining equipment for his Philippines forces. He also failed, but did gain assurances from the Navy Department that they would develop the type of torpedo boat MacArthur had requested. Quezon and party moved on to Mexico City where MacArthur unintentionally upstaged the Philippine president. Next on the agenda was Europe, but MacArthur instead returned to the United States with Davis. He had other matters to tend to.

First was his mother's funeral. Pinky's remains were brought to Arlington Cemetery for burial next to her husband. It was a simple ceremony attended by her son, Secretary of War Woodring, and a handful of close friends. Pershing was not there but sent a floral arrangement and MacArthur said, "Nothing could have pleased my mother more."[1]

An even bigger event occurred on April 30—Douglas and Jean married. It was a civil ceremony performed by a deputy city clerk in the New York Municipal Building. Only Davis and Hutter were present. There was no honeymoon. MacArthur took off to accompany Quezon to Mexico City and Washington, while Jean returned home to Murfreesboro before the newlyweds returned to Manila to begin their lives as Mr. and Mrs. MacArthur.

Jean and Douglas seemed to have a perfect marriage. She

referred to her husband as "General" and with her Southern accent it came out sounding like "Gin'ral." Jean also called him "Sir Boss," after a character in Dickens's *A Connecticut Yankee in King Arthur's Court*. He called her "Ma'am," so she wouldn't forget her Southern roots. Unlike Louise, Jean approved of army life and had a great compassion for those who served their country.

In *Reminiscences* MacArthur described his marriage to Jean in a very matter-of-fact way. "It was perhaps the smartest thing I have ever done," he wrote, "she has been my constant friend, sweetheart and devoted supporter every since. How she has been able to put up with my eccentricities and crochets all these years is quite beyond my comprehension. She was a rebel when I met her and she still is."[2]

Ten months after their wedding, Arthur IV was born February 21, 1938, at Sternberg Hospital, Manila. His parents called him "Junior." He was baptized on his grandfather's birthday, June 2, in an Episcopalian ceremony witnessed by the Quezons, who served as godparents. Douglas and Jean were assisted in raising their son by Loh Chiu, a Chinese *amah*, nicknamed "Ah Cheu" by the MacArthurs. By all accounts the MacArthurs had a very happy home.

Fatherhood suited MacArthur well. He was a doting father and very protective of his son, whom he called "Sergeant." When young Arthur was old enough to walk, his father would march with him throughout their home, joyfully executing childlike drills and commands. Then Arthur followed his father into the bathroom, and while MacArthur shaved, they would duet the few barracks songs Arthur knew by heart. MacArthur was reported to be overly protective of his son. For example, when Arthur was older he broke his arm ice skating. MacArthur visited him five times a day in the hospital.

Socially, MacArthur was a bit of a hermit, but enjoyed the company of the Filipino people more than the company of the Americans living in the Philippines. He liked talking to them about spirituality, patriotism, morality, and Christianity. He was sixty years old now, but looked twenty years younger. He rarely exercised these days except for a few calisthenics in the morning and long walks later in the day. MacArthur was a very simple man when it came to life's pleasures. He liked plain food three times a day. He never drank coffee and limited his alcoholic intake to one predinner cocktail, a gimlet (gin and lime juice).

His one vice was smoking. MacArthur smoked a pack a day, using one of his many carved ivory cigarette holders. And after dinner he enjoyed a large Corona cigar. Later in life he began to puff on a pipe and, along with his field marshal cap, it became part of the MacArthur persona. When he did leave his home, MacArthur loved going to the movies and frequented Manila's six theaters that showed first-run films. His favorites were Westerns, but he pretty much saw whatever was playing.

Eisenhower and Ord saw very little of MacArthur. As chief of staff in Washington he could be counted on to put in long, strenuous hours. In the Philippines he relied more on staffers and advisers. His routine was to arrive in his office around 11:00 a.m., work a few hours, then take a long lunch and work a few more hours before returning home. Occasionally he came back to the office and worked a few hours in the evening. MacArthur always worked seven days a week and never took days off or a full vacation.

After three years in the Philippines, MacArthur's relations with its president deteriorated. Quezon became disillusioned with the defense program MacArthur created. The program was draining his country financially and Quezon's advisers told him that the defense plan was creating a false sense of security. He reiterated harsh feelings in a speech before a large audience in Manila: "The Philippines could not be defended even if every last Filipino were armed with modern weapons."[3]

MacArthur also clashed with Ord and Eisenhower. In one instance he insisted that a number of Filipino army units be assembled for a national parade through the streets of Manila as a means of invigorating public morale. MacArthur had not discussed, much less cleared, his idea with Quezon; and when Ord and Eisenhower informed him that their budget could not possibly stand such a hit without sacrificing funds needed to carry out more important projects, the pair was summarily overruled.

When Quezon learned of the plan, he conveyed his displeasure to MacArthur. Embarrassed by the matter, MacArthur lamely denied he had ever ordered his staff to proceed. Ord and Eisenhower were the chief scapegoats. The parade was duly canceled, but the bad feelings between MacArthur and his two assistants were heightened. "Never again were we on the same warm and cordial terms,"[4] recalled Eisenhower. Nevertheless, in early 1938 Eisenhower willingly agreed to a one-year extension in Manila at the urging of both Quezon and MacArthur, a decision made more out of loyalty to the president than allegiance to MacArthur.

Then in 1939 Quezon requested that the National Assembly establish a Department of National Defense, which undermined MacArthur's authority. Quezon was also pushing Washington for early independence, but that request fell on deaf ears. Relations between Quezon and MacArthur were now so bad that the Philippine president most often turned to Eisenhower and Ord for advice. The longer MacArthur remained in Manila the more distanced he became from Quezon. It became obvious it was time to leave.

Tension also increased between Quezon and Roosevelt, and MacArthur was stuck in the middle and grew uncomfortable about the situation. He felt more of an allegiance to Quezon and offered his resignation to Roosevelt, who tried to pacify him with command of Hawaii and the West Coast, but MacArthur turned down the office and left the army as a four-star general. The president gladly accepted MacArthur's resignation and told him in a carefully worded message: "With great reluctance and deep regret I have approved your application for retirement effective December 31. Personally, as well as officially, I want to thank you for your outstanding services to our country. Your record in war and in peace is a brilliant chapter of American history."[5]

MacArthur thought he could remain in the Philippines after his retirement as military adviser, but the country's legislature didn't want him. Some still had doubts about his expensive defense program, while others did not like the fact he was earning a salary of $36,000 a year. But Quezon stepped in and supported him by issuing an executive proclamation declaring that MacArthur would continue as Philippine military adviser. Back in Washington he was abandoned. Secretary of War Woodring told Roosevelt that MacArthur was now an employee of the Philippine government and "is no longer a representative of the United States."[6]

Meanwhile on September 1, 1939, Hitler's German war machine attacked Poland and after a brief struggle overran the country. Two years before Japan had attacked China again, this time more brutally than before. Now the world was at war again. Eisenhower returned to the United States to work on war planning, despite a valiant effort by MacArthur to keep him in the Philippines. He told his boss: "General, in my opinion the United States cannot remain out of this war for long. I want to go home as soon as possible. I want to participate in the preparatory work that I'm sure is going to be intense."[7]

MacArthur believed Eisenhower was "making a mistake, and that the work he was doing in the Philippines was far more important than any I [Eisenhower] could do as a mere lieutenant colonel in the American Army."[8] MacArthur could not have been more incorrect. The two heroes of World War II would not see each other again until several years later when Eisenhower visited Japan in May 1946. Later Eisenhower reflected on his time in the Philippines and declared that he was "deeply grateful for the administrative experience gained under General MacArthur" that helped prepare him for "the great responsibilities of the war period."[9]

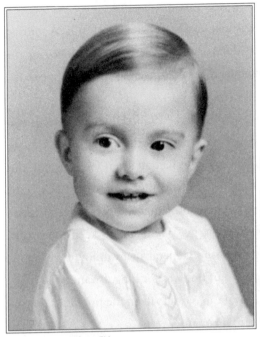

Arthur MacArthur IV.

MacArthur, Jean and Arthur IV leaving the Capitol (1951).

Jean Marie Faircloth.

TWELVE

There Is a War to Be Won

LIEUTENANT COLONEL RICHARD K. Sutherland took Eisenhower's place as chief of staff. A veteran of the AEF and numerous troop assignments, Sutherland was devoted to MacArthur through World War II and acted as his bulldog when subordinates were found not performing to the commander's satisfaction. Despite the respect he earned from his staff, according to one of MacArthur's biographers they were put off "by his nasty temper, brusqueness, and autocratic manner." Sutherland was also a charter member of what was later called the "Bataan Gang," a small cadre of officers who served with MacArthur in the Philippines and Southwest Pacific campaigns, as well as during the occupation of Japan. He relied heavily on the Bataan Gang in the months ahead as the Philippines prepared for the inevitable.

By early 1941 all signs indicated the United States and Japan were heading toward war. Diplomatic discussions between the two countries continued until December of that year, but they were proving fruitless. MacArthur was more optimistic, believing Japan would be foolish to go to war against the United States, since the British and Dutch would join forces to crush Japan. They had been fighting in China for about four years and MacArthur said the combat had "eaten into the foundation of the highly complex economic and military structure of Japan."[2] But if he was wrong and the United States did go to war, MacArthur wanted a significant say in how it was fought.

That January MacArthur made it known it was time to come out of retirement. In a letter to Roosevelt's press secretary, Stephen I. Early, MacArthur suggested that the president return him to active duty as commander of forces in the Far East. There was no immediate reaction from Roosevelt, so MacArthur wrote to Early again, as well as army chief of staff George C. Marshall, some months later. He told both of them his desire to shut down the military mission, return to the United States, and live in San Antonio unless there was a reason to stay in the Philippines. Marshall responded by reassuring MacArthur that although the decision to the leave the Philippines was his alone, the situation in the Far East was of great concern and Roosevelt would recall him to active duty when he saw fit.

That day arrived July 26, 1941. President Roosevelt reacted to Japan's deployment of thirty thousand troops in Saigon and Haiphong in Indochina by issuing a decree to freeze all Japanese assets in the United States, closing the Panama Canal to Japanese shipping, and placing an embargo on the export of raw materials to Japan. Even more significant, the president signed orders placing the Philippine army into the service of the United States and establishing a new Far East Command. MacArthur would lead it with the rank of major general. The official name was the United States Army Force Far East (USAFFE).

MacArthur was back in Roosevelt's good graces, who two days later promoted him to temporary lieutenant general. Telegrams poured into MacArthur's office from friends and strangers in the Philippines and the United States. At sixty-one, he entered a new phase of his career. Many people at this age think of retirement, and although the general had seriously considered leaving the military, command of USAFFE was just what he needed to boost his morale. Another commander shared collateral duties with MacArthur on the Philippines, Admiral Thomas C. Hart. A veteran of the U.S. Navy since the Spanish-American War, Hart was in command of the weak Asiatic Fleet that consisted of three cruisers, thirteen destroyers, eighteen submarines, and a halfdozen PT boats.

After years of neglect the United States was now making an effort to defend the Philippines against Japanese invasion, or so MacArthur, Quezon, and everyone else on the islands believed. There was good reason to be optimistic. By July 31, 1941, the Philippine Department consisted of 22,000 troops, about 12,000 of them Philippine Scouts. The main component was the Philippine Division, under the command of Major General Jonathan M. Wainwright. Another 8,500 reinforcements arrived between July and December.

Most remarkably MacArthur's requests for equipment were

granted and by November a backlog of 1.1 million tons of material intended for the Philippines had accumulated in U.S. ports and depots awaiting vessels. MacArthur estimated that once he received all of the necessary supplies and troops, it would take until early April 1942 before the defenses in the Philippines would be ready to repulse an invasion. And based on his earlier prediction about the Japanese forces, he firmly believed he had that much time. But word from the War Department told him otherwise.

In late November a strongly worded alert from the War Department was radioed to all commands: "Negotiations with Japan appear terminated, Japanese future action unpredictable, but hostile action possible at any moment. If hostilities cannot, repeat, cannot be avoided the United desires Japan commit the first act." Additionally, MacArthur's message was appended with instructions to implement Rainbow Five, a war plan that gave him authority to conduct air raids against enemy forces and installations within tactical range.

December 7, 1941, all the speculations and the preparations for war were cast aside. No more guessing if or when the Japanese were going to attack. On a Sunday morning, a date President Roosevelt declared "would live in infamy," 350 enemy planes approached the U.S. naval base at Pearl Harbor, Hawaii, and the military bases on Oahu undetected. They attacked for just a few hours but their accuracy was devastating. The tally of U.S. losses was 4 battleships and 180 aircraft destroyed, along with 2,400 sailors killed, while the Japanese Imperial Navy lost a mere 29 aircraft and 55 pilots. The attack was a complete surprise and the Americans proved any easy target.

At 4:00 a.m. on December 8, MacArthur and Jean were asleep in their Manila apartment when Sutherland called to relay the news about the attack, which was still in progress since the Philippines were nineteen hours ahead of Hawaii. Sutherland had learned of the attack from Brigadier General Spencer B. Atkin, MacArthur's Signal Corps chief, who was told by one of his staff, who heard the news while tuned to a California radio station.[3] The exact time the news about Pearl Harbor reached the Philippines is unclear.

Although not entirely surprised by what his chief of staff had just told him, MacArthur recognized the enormity of the situation; and as he always did in situations like this, he turned to God. He pulled out a Bible that he inherited from Pinky and read for a short while. This gave the general some solace, but needing more comfort, he put down the Bible and prayed. Then he headed to his headquarters and met with his staff.

Believing at first that the Japanese attack had been unsuccessful, MacArthur remained calm and waited for further news. That came from Brigadier General Leonard Gerow at the War Plans Division, who told him the attack was indeed crippling and MacArthur should expect an air raid at any time. Meanwhile, General Marshall ordered MacArthur to execute the existing war plan, Rainbow Five. But MacArthur did not comply, and from this point there is confusion over what happened that day. It is clear that within the first few hours after the Pearl Harbor attack was reported, a USAFFE response was delayed because MacArthur did not want to overreact until he had more information at hand.

Brigadier General Lewis Brereton, on the other hand,

wanted to immediately bomb the Japanese airfields at Formosa. MacArthure had selected Brereton at the end of October to command the Far East Air Force, or FEAF, as it was known. It was a crucial component of USAFFE, since unlike before, the Philippine air defenses were now a top priority. Air warning and air defense systems were primitive and it would require significant work to make them useful.

When Brereton came on board in November 1941 he literally had to start from scratch. Neglect through the years had rendered most of the Philippine airfields useless. Several fields were scattered throughout the islands, but only one, Clark, was capable of handling the B-17 Flying Fortress bombers. The B-17s were one of the Air Corps' newest weapons and Washington sent them to the Philippines as a deterrent against Japanese aggression. Brereton accomplished a lot in a short time, but like MacArthur, thought he had until spring of the following year to build FEAF into a first-class operation. At Brereton's disposal were 8,100 U.S. Army Air Forces personnel, mostly at Clark on Luzon, with another 500 at Del Monte on Mindanao.[4]

In the days leading up to Pearl Harbor, Brereton had concentrated on preparing Clark Field for a possible attack. What concerned him the most were the nineteen heavy B-17s at Clark, the heart and soul of FEAF, that were like sitting ducks. Brereton had considered sending all of the heavy bombers to Del Monte, but only two squadrons were sent. Later he said the reason for this decision was based upon the promise that the 7th Bombardment Group was being sent to the Philippines and they would be stationed at Del Monte. Had he moved all of the B-17s to that field there would have been no room for other planes.[5] MacArthur had also weighed in the necessity of keeping his heavy bombers safe. On November 29 he wrote to Marshall that "the location of potential enemy fields and types of aircraft indicate that heavy bombers should be located south of Luzon where they would be reasonably safe from attack."[6]

Meanwhile, Brereton pressed for his B-17s to attack the Japanese airfields in Formosa and called MacArthur's chief of staff, Sutherland, to ask permission. The answer was no. At this time USAFFE was on the defensive and MacArthur was trying to determine why the Japanese had not yet launched an attack on the Philippines. They would have, if fog over Formosa had not delayed their planes taking off.

Later that morning Brereton again requested that his B-17s be allowed to target Formosa. He did not have specific targets in mind, but could find some supply ships to bomb. This time MacArthur told him to "hold off for the present." It was clear from this response that MacArthur was also getting impatient. Finally at quarter past ten he gave Brereton permission to make a reconnaissance flight over Formosa to find potential targets and then to launch a B-17 attack that afternoon if feasible. MacArthur initially seemed not to grasp the urgency of the situation, but later that day he began to recognize that the B-17s were valuable to use against the Japanese if he acted quickly.

The news that the Japanese had indeed bombed the Philippines at Baguio, about one hundred miles north of Manila, reversed MacArthur's decision. Then word was received that the harbor at Davao and a radio station at Aparri were struck. While all of this was happening, Brereton sent all but three of his B-17s at Clark airborne, in the event that the Japanese attacked that morning. They were about to run out of fuel and he called them back to Clark. Once on the ground they were to be refueled and then sent on their way to bomb Formosa.

For USAFFE this change in direction was too late. At 12:30 on December 8, the Japanese Eleventh Air Fleet flew overhead and attacked Clark Field and the nearby fighter base at Iba Field. Just as at Pearl Harbor, the Japanese had an easy time and they destroyed or disabled 18 of Far East Air Force's 35 B-17s, 53 of its 107 P-40s, 3 P-35s, and more than 25 other aircraft. Structures at both fields were severely damaged, and there were significant casualties—80 killed and 150 wounded. Additional attacks during the next few days destroyed what remained of FEAF's planes.

Needless to say, MacArthur's reaction was one of dismay. On the first day of war he had lost air superiority, which effectively meant the loss of the Philippines was a foregone conclusion. He never publicly blamed Brereton. In *Reminiscences*, MacArthur defended his FEAF commander by pointing out:

> Our air force in the Philippines contained many antiquated models, and were hardly more than a token force with insufficient equipment, incompleted fields, and inadequate maintenance. The force was in process of integration, radar defenses were not yet operative, and the personnel was raw and inexperienced. They were hopelessly outnumbered and never had a chance of winning.[7]

MacArthur was correct. Even if Brereton had been able to launch his B-17s against the Japanese at Formosa, no one knows how effective they would have been. Because the Japanese had a superior air force, without the addition of more planes and crew, FEAF was fighting a losing battle anyway. Previous biographers have taken MacArthur to task for not immediately reacting to the Pearl Harbor attack and ordering an air strike against Japanese airbases in Formosa as Rainbow Five gave him the authority to undertake. Such criticism is warranted.

MacArthur was commander of the forces in the Philippines and should have insured that preparations were at hand to remove his aircraft from harm's way once it was obvious war had broken out. He was as much at fault as the army and navy commanders at Pearl who didn't do nearly enough to prepare their bases for an attack. Brereton, on the other hand, as the air commander should have been more forceful with MacArthur and deserves at least some of the blame for the debacle at Clark and Iba fields. It should also be stressed that blame is placed on the War Department as well for basing war plans on the belief that Japan was not capable of attacking until 1942. The warning signs that Japan was gearing up for war were visible, but no one paid attention to them.

During the next few weeks it was a losing battle for FEAF, and USAFFE for that matter. Brereton tried desperately to reorganize, but it was a vain attempt. Japanese planes freely attacked the Philippines and destroyed more airfields and the Cavite Naval Station south of Manila. Brereton was continually losing more planes. Exasperated, he received MacArthur's permission to move the remaining B-17s and other combat aircraft to Darwin,

Australia. On December 24 Brereton and his FEAF headquarters headed south.

Rear Admiral Thomas C. Hart, who commanded the Asiatic Fleet, also departed the Philippines around this time. Relations between MacArthur and Hart had been strained for some time for a variety of reasons, such as, jurisdiction over offshore air patrol, which the admiral claimed MacArthur interfered with. They also bickered over incidents involving soldiers and sailors at Shanghai and Hong Kong. The final straw occurred when the twenty-nine submarines under Hart's command failed to have any impact on the Japanese invading Lingayen Gulf. MacArthur had had enough. He also felt that Hart did little to assist in defending the islands after the air force was lost. Hart left Manila on Christmas Day for the Malay Barrier, where his fleet joined the British and Dutch forces.

Heading toward the Philippines at a rapid pace was the Japanese Fourteenth Army, commanded by Lieutenant General Masaharu Homma and forty-three thousand troops who were fresh from combat in China. They were escorted by a naval flotilla consisting of two battleships and eight cruisers. At dawn on December 22 the Japanese arrived at the beaches of Lingayen. Their only real opposition was heavy rain and high seas. A few American planes and submarines were close by, along with a Philippine Scout cavalry regiment and three Philippine army divisions, but they were no match for Homma's forces and the Japanese easily secured the beachhead.

Homma's veterans made short work of the beach defenders and moved down Route 3 toward Manila. By the afternoon of December 23, Wainwright realized that the Japanese could not be stopped unless he formed a new defensive line. The first natural barrier was the Agno River, which ran east to west some twenty miles south of the Lingayen beaches. Wainwright received permission from Sutherland to withdraw to the river.

Wainwright's troops were the targets of continual Japanese attacks. The more skillful enemy overwhelmed them and the defenders had to withdraw. MacArthur, for now, still believed that his forces could make a defensive stand until reinforcements arrived. The troops had been fighting on half rations for two weeks, however, and were now in a weakened state. MacArthur told his commanders that he was "very much displeased" at reports that the troops were in need of relief, and that he wanted such reports to cease because they were hurting morale. But behind the scenes he knew the island fortress of Corregidor represented the best hope for holding out until help arrived, and for that reason MacArthur had already begun sending food stocks to the island.

MacArthur's faith at this time had never been stronger. Along with divine intervention, and some optimistic cables from Roosevelt and Marshall, he believed that it was just a matter of time before reinforcements arrived. "Help is definitely on the way," he told his officers. But in actuality no help was heading to the Philippines.

Unbeknownst to MacArthur, Roosevelt had made a pact with Prime Minister Winston Churchill in a Washington conference after the Pearl Harbor attack that the European Theater would come first. Until victory was at hand there, strategy in the Pacific Theater was to contain the Japanese. Marshall also supported this policy despite his supportive communiqués to MacArthur that indicated otherwise. "I was not informed of any of these vital conferences," MacArthur wrote, "and believed that a brave effort at relief was in the making."[8]

MacArthur and Lt. General Jonathan Wainwright greet each other for the first time since parting at Corregidor more than three years before (1945).

MacArthur stands on the balcony of his office at City Hall, Manila, Luzon, Philippines Islands.

THIRTEEN

Withdrawal

As EACH DAY passed, so did hope for relief. With reality setting in, MacArthur reluctantly told Wainwright that War Plan Orange was now in place. Before, MacArthur had put little thought into Orange since he assumed that the Philippine army would be fully trained before Japan attacked and viewed the plan and its creators as defeatist. MacArthur believed he could defend all of Luzon, if not the entire Philippines, and told Wainwright a few days after Pearl Harbor that the northern Luzon beaches were to be held "at all costs." Now circumstances changed that line of thinking. Wainwright's forces to the north and south of Manila would immediately withdraw to the Bataan Peninsula. Thirty miles long and fifteen miles wide, the peninsula was heavily forested and jutted toward the island-fort of Corregidor to the south.

Part of the withdrawal called for the Southern Luzon Force, commanded by Major General George M. Parker Jr., to move north of Manila and join Wainwright on Bataan. MacArthur hoped that Bataan and Corregidor could be defended until the promised reinforcements arrived from the United States. MacArthur's decision to use War Plan Orange put a heavy burden on Luzon's defenders. Besides stipulating an orderly withdrawal to defensive positions on Bataan, it required the stockpiling of supplies and the preparation of new defenses. To allow time for supplies to be moved to Bataan and for Parker's force to work its way north, MacArthur ordered Wainwright to withdraw south through a series of defensive lines. Each was to be held long enough to force the Japanese to halt and deploy; when the enemy attacked in force, the defenders were to withdraw to the next line. It was a game of cat and mouse, and MacArthur wanted it completed by January 8, only two weeks away.

Wainwright's retreat to Bataan was spectacular. Because U.S. Army regiments were being held in reserve, most of his troops consisted of Philippine units, some led by American officers. While Wainwright organized his forces, Japanese commander Homma was unsure whether to attack Bataan or press on to Manila. Regardless, his delay gave Parker time to move north. By New Year's Day, Wainwright's men were in their last defensive line, where his three under-strength divisions had the task of delaying the Japanese long enough for the Southern Luzon Force to cross into Bataan. Success was at hand. By January 6, two days before MacArthur's deadline, more than 80,000 troops and 25,000 refugees had reached Bataan.

On Bataan, Wainwright's forces were far from secure. In late January the Japanese pressed forward and a series of bloody engagements ensued. With the Americans and Filipinos in a defensive position and having the upper hand, they managed to inflict heavy losses on the Japanese. For most of the next two months Homma's forces held back because they were having their own supply problems. This allowed the Americans and Filipinos to prepare an intricate system of tunnels and defensive entrenchments in an attempt to counter the anticipated Japanese offensive.

While in a holding pattern, conditions became desperate. A dwindling food supply weakened the Americans and Filipinos by the day. Eventually, MacArthur—over the objections of the American commanders—ordered a reduction of the daily ration on Bataan to three-eighths of a standard ration. There was some relief in February when several interisland steamers from the southern Philippines snuck by Japan's blockade to bring small amounts of food and other supplies.

Beyond the halls of the War Department, Jonathan Wainwright was largely unknown to most Americans, who were also kept in the dark about the perilous circumstances on Bataan. All they knew, based on daily newspaper accounts, was that General MacArthur was in charge and that was to his liking. It was no secret that MacArthur enjoyed the notoriety and press. From his headquarters he issued regular news bulletins portraying the heroic defense of the Filipino-American forces. More importantly, however, MacArthur wanted the world to know that he was handling the situation, and whatever the end result, he was fully responsible for either success or failure. But back in Washington

Roosevelt and Marshall didn't feel so comfortable. They were unwilling to commit full-scale reinforcement to the Philippines, and it was obvious to them that surrender was inevitable. And if that were the case, MacArthur had to be evacuated before he fell into enemy hands.

With the Japanese approaching, MacArthur had remained in Manila as long as possible, but the city was no longer safe, so he moved his headquarters to Corregidor on December 25. Reminiscent of when he served on the Western Front in 1918, air attacks by the Japanese destroyed all the exposed structures on the island, forcing the movement of USAFFE headquarters into the Malinta Tunnel. Constructed on top of Malinta Hill by the Army Corps of Engineers from 1922 to 1932, it first served as a bombproof storage facility, but was later converted into a hospi-tal. Eventually most of the headquarters moved to Bataan, leaving only the nucleus with MacArthur. He described his new office as "bare, glaringly lighted, and containing only the essential furni-ture and equipment for administrative procedure."[1]

From the tunnel MacArthur directed USAFFE, but to the men who were exposed to the elements and subjected to enemy attack at any time, it gave the impression their commander was hid-ing. Those who had fought beside MacArthur during World War I knew better. He was fearless and was much more comfortable confronting the enemy than hiding from it. Nevertheless, he unfairly earned the moniker of "Dugout Doug," which inspired a ballad to the tune of "The Battle Hymn of the Republic."

Joining MacArthur on Corregidor were his wife and son. Jean and Arthur put up a brave front despite the constant shelling and difficulty of living in a tunnel. Frequently MacArthur and his wife were observed walking throughout the defenses, meeting the gun crews and offering words of encouragement. MacArthur often left the tunnel during bombing and shelling, never displaying signs of fear. He was reliving World War I—not what one expected from a general nicknamed "Dugout Doug." Quezon learned of MacArthur's exposure to enemy fire and was appalled. He wrote MacArthur to remind him that "you owe it to your government and your people, as well as to my government and people, to take no unnecessary risks because if something should happen to you the effect upon the armed forces and civilian population of the Philippines would be, to say the least, most demoralizing."[2]

In Washington the War Department and the president were also concerned about MacArthur's safety. Not willing to risk having the USAFFE commander killed or captured, in February, Roosevelt ordered him to leave Corregidor for Australia. The evacuation order was not only a blow to his ego, but MacArthur still held out hope that somehow the Philippines could be defended and the Japanese defeated. He wasn't given a choice and plans were set into motion to remove him from danger.

At the south dock of Corregidor's Bottomside, MacArthur met with Wainwright for the last time in the Philippines. Wainwright had been a plebe at West Point when MacArthur was a first classman. Concerned about how his image would be affected when news broke that he was vacating the Philippines, MacArthur wanted Wainwright to make clear to the soldiers that he was leaving only on the direct order of the president. He would return with reinforcements as soon as he could; meanwhile, the Americans must hold out. MacArthur told him, "Jim [one of Wainwright's nicknames] hold on till I come back for you." Before they said good-bye MacArthur gave Wainwright a box of cigars and two jars of shaving cream.

On March 12 MacArthur, his family, including Ah Cheu, and seventeen servicemen left Corregidor aboard PT boats under the command of Lieutenant John D. Bulkeley. Their destination was the southern island of Mindanao. Each passenger could bring only one suitcase weighing no more than thirty-five pounds. The MacArthurs brought very little with them, mostly just the clothes on their backs. Provisions consisted of what Jean and Sidney Huff, MacArthur's naval adviser, could gather into four duffel bags—mainly canned salmon and orangeade. One oddity that Bulkeley allowed was a mattress for the MacArthurs, so there was some element of comfort in what was expected to be a rough trip.

Bulkeley's squadron of four boats was beat up after weeks of continuous action and could go no faster than 17 knots. It was a 900 kilometer trip that took two days through enemy infested waters and the boats encountered several close calls with Japanese submarines. They finally arrived at daybreak on March 14 and were escorted to Del Monte Field. Awaiting the MacArthur party was a B-17, dispatched from Australia by Lieutenant General George H. Brett, commander of United States Air Forces in Australia (USAFIA).

There were supposed to be others, but two had failed to arrive and the third crashed. MacArthur refused to board the remaining plane, considering it unfit to carry passengers and told Brett to send three more. Unsure if there were suitable planes available in Australia, MacArthur radioed Marshall and made the same request of the chief of staff. "The best three planes in the United States or Hawaii should be made available," MacArthur demanded, "with completely adequate and experienced crews. To attempt such a desperate and important trip with inadequate equipment would amount to consigning the whole party to death and I could not accept such responsibility."[3]

His message was heard, loud and clear. Three B-17s were sent immediately from Darwin, but only two made it to Del Monte around midnight of March 16. The other had to turn back because of engine trouble. Two planes would have to be enough, but they were overloaded and the passengers had to abandon their luggage, although the mattress was allowed. The trip to Australia was as traumatic as the journey in the PT boats. While preparing to land in Darwin, a Japanese air raid diverted the flight to a nearby airstrip at Batchelor Field, about sixty miles south of Darwin. MacArthur arrived there on March 17 and then, despite Jean's pleading of no more plane rides, the party was forced to travel the next leg on a C-47 because Japanese bombers were heading toward Batchelor.

After four more hours of flying they landed in Alice Springs, a small town in the center of Australia. There were no trains available to take the party to Adelaide, so a special one was called up that wouldn't arrive until the next afternoon. Worn out, everyone stayed in an old hotel that was plagued with flies. The train ride to Adelaide was only slightly better than the trip by PT boat and B-17. There were constant interruptions as the train stopped frequently and didn't arrive at its destination until seventy hours later. During one stop at Terowie, a small railway township in South Australia, a reporter asked MacArthur for a statement. Off the cuff he responded, "I came out of Bataan and I shall return."

When they finally reached the Adelaide station, MacArthur was greeted by more reporters who also wanted a statement. Never one to shy away from the press, MacArthur complied and expanded on the comment he had made earlier with a slight deviation. Reading from notes he took on the back of an envelope, he said "The President of the United States ordered me to break through the Japanese lines, and proceed from Corregidor to Australia for the purpose, as I understand it, of organizing the American offensive against Japan, a primary object of which is the relief of the Philippines. I came through and I shall return."[4]

He had changed *Bataan* to *through* for greater emphasis. Washington was not happy that MacArthur had referred only to himself and asked that he amend his promise to "We shall return." He ignored the request. MacArthur's assurance that he would return to the Philippines became the rallying cry for the Pacific and a boost the worried American people desperately needed. Those three words were as strong as "Remember the Maine" that his father had heard forty-four years before.

Before leaving the Philippines, MacArthur designated Wainwright as his successor, but only for those troops on Bataan and Corregidor. He thought this through carefully because the plan was to direct a defense of the Philippines from Australia. MacArthur established four separate commands for Bataan, Corregidor, and two groups of southern islands. The War Department, which had not been informed of MacArthur's plan for independent commands, told Wainwright on March 20 that he had been promoted to lieutenant general and that he commanded all U.S. forces in the Philippines. He was nominally part of MacArthur's new theater but was authorized to communicate directly with Washington.

While MacArthur was safely in Australia on March 28, Wainwright told the War Department that food stocks on Bataan would be exhausted by April 15, hinting that surrender was eminent. On April 4, MacArthur cabled Wainwright that "under no conditions" should he surrender. "If food fails, you will prepare and execute an attack upon the enemy." Wainwright replied that his troops were "so weak from malnutrition that they have no power of resistance."[5]

But orders were orders, and Wainwright passed on MacArthur's demand for an attack. Major General Edward P. King Jr., in command at Bataan, received Wainwright's orders, but refused to obey them. He knew that his soldiers were weak from starvation and sickness; attacking was out of the question. Without informing Wainwright, on the morning of April 9, King surrendered his Luzon force of more than 70,000 U.S. and Philippine troops to the Japanese.

MacArthur was furious when he heard of the surrender and demanded an explanation. Wainwright acknowledged King had not told him that he was going to capitulate, but agreed that it was the right course of action because of conditions on Bataan. He cabled President Roosevelt, "I have done all that could have been done to hold Bataan, but starved men without air and with inadequate field artillery support cannot endure the terrific aerial and artillery bombardment that my troops were subjected to."[6]

Corregidor was next for the Japanese and they moved their heaviest artillery to positions close to the island. From there they launched three weeks of intense bombardment that destroyed most of the U.S. artillery emplacements. On the night of May 5, Homma landed a regiment on the northern tip of the island. The defenders held on and inflicted heavy losses on the Japanese, but it didn't prevent them from consolidating their beachheads and bringing tanks and artillery ashore. The end was near.

On May 6, Wainwright ordered a white flag raised above his headquarters. He cabled President Roosevelt that he was arranging the terms of surrender later that day. The earlier surrender of 70,000 American and Filipino troops on Bataan a month earlier, and now the surrender of 13,000 more on Corregidor made it the largest capitulation of American troops in U.S. history.

Wainwright began more than three years as Japan's highest-ranking American prisoner. MacArthur's reaction to the surrender was one of disbelief. He sent a cable to the War Department that he believed Wainwright to have become "temporarily unbalanced." Washington disagreed, and on July 30, 1942, Marshall told MacArthur that Wainwright was to be awarded the Medal of Honor. MacArthur was furious, informing Marshall that such an award would be an injustice to unnamed generals who had "exhibited powers of leadership and inspiration to a degree greatly superior to that of General Wainwright."[7] Although neither Marshall nor Secretary of War Henry L. Stimson thought much of this response, they didn't want to create hostility with MacArthur and shelved the Medal of Honor idea.

FOURTEEN

In Australia

BEFORE THE MACARTHUR party left for Melbourne, news of the American general's arrival spread, and large crowds descended upon the rail station shouting, "Welcome to Australia!" This was the best thing he heard all day. Earlier he met with USAFFE assistant chief of staff, Brigadier General Richard A. Marshall, who told MacArthur the grim news: there were only about 25,000 American troops and less than 250 combat aircraft in Australia. Marshall continued briefing him on the way to Adelaide and nothing MacArthur learned was positive. Chief among the issues were Australia's weak defenses. There was only one Australian division to guard the homeland. The others were supporting British forces in the Middle East. "God have mercy on us!" MacArthur exclaimed. Those on the train to

Melbourne said he paced back and forth all night in his private coach.

They arrived in Melbourne on March 21 and were greeted by a crowd estimated at between 4,000 and 6,000 Australians. This was in addition to a 360-man American honor guard, about sixty correspondents, and a host of Australian dignitaries. MacArthur was led to a waiting microphone where he captivated his audience with a brilliant speech. He first praised the bravery of the Australian soldier, but made it clear that "success in modern war requires something more than courage and a willingness to die . . . No general can make something out of nothing. My success or failure will depend primarily upon the resources which respective governments place at my disposal."[1] Now it was time to go to work. Jean and Arthur went shopping to replenish the family wardrobe and the MacArthurs settled in to their new life down under.

On April 18, 1942, MacArthur was appointed Supreme Commander of Allied Forces in the Southwest Pacific Area (SWPA). This included Australia, the Philippines, the Solomons, New Guinea, the Bismark Achipelago, Borneo, and all of the Netherland Indies except for Sumatra.[2] Within SWPA's command structure was Lieutenant General George Brett, commander of the Allied Air Forces, and Vice Admiral Herbert F. Leary, commander of the Allied Naval Forces. Holdovers from USAFFE such as Sutherland as chief of staff, Marshall as deputy chief of staff, and Willoughby as his G-2 or intelligence officer, were with MacArthur in Australia. Since the bulk of land forces in the theater were Australian, General Marshall insisted an Australian be appointed as Commander, Allied Land Forces, and the job went to General Sir Thomas Blamey. Although predominantly Australian and American, MacArthur's command also included small numbers of personnel from the Netherlands East Indies, the United Kingdom, and other countries.

Initially located in Melbourne, the SWPA headquarters was moved to Brisbane in July because it provided better communications facilities. MacArthur established a close relationship with the prime minister of Australia, John Curtin, who was instrumental in helping secure more resources for SWPA and for promoting the American general as the savior of Australia. June 13 was declared MacArthur Day and it was celebrated in all of the major cities with speeches and rallies. Two months later an opinion poll conducted by a Sydney newspaper declared MacArthur hands down as the most important public figure in Australia. An Australian fighter pilot requested that MacArthur be the godfather of his newborn son, and the general said yes. The Japanese, on the other hand, tried to counter the adulation with radio broadcasts and propaganda leaflets that portrayed MacArthur as a coward who had abandoned his men in the Philippines.

Back home the MacArthur craze was at its pinnacle and continued well after the war ended. It started when news broke of the evacuation to Bataan and his popularity only increased when stories of his daring trip to Australia were told. His every move was covered by newspapers and devoured by the adoring public. MacArthur's image adorned everything from magazine covers to lapel buttons. Countless newborns throughout the United States were given "Douglas" as their first or middle name. Roads and streets were renamed "MacArthur." Even City Park, the area in Little Rock, Arkansas, where he was born, was renamed "MacArthur Park."

An Indian tribe adopted him as an honorary member and the University of Wisconsin conferred the honorary degree of Doctor of Laws during their spring commencement in absentia. New York publishing houses hopped on the MacArthur bandwagon by producing hastily written biographies that only added to his allure. One such book was a compilation of his prewar speeches and reports that emphasized his strong beliefs in patriotism and religion. More monumental was the talk of MacArthur as a challenger to Roosevelt in the upcoming election. He had heard this before. In 1936 he had not wanted to be president, nor did the 1944 Republican nomination appeal to him now. MacArthur was in the midst of war and he could better serve his country in the Pacific Theater, not in the White House.

SWPA's first task was to prevent an invasion of Australia. MacArthur decided the best course of action was to go on the offensive and attack the Japanese at New Guinea. Meanwhile, from June 3 to 6, 1942, strategy in the Pacific Theater changed when the U.S. Navy soundly defeated their Japanese opponents, first at Midway, then at Coral Sea. From this point the Japanese Imperial Navy was never the same, but far from defeated. The Japanese now concentrated on Milne Bay, New Guinea, with the ultimate goal of capturing Port Moresby by way of the unwelcoming Owen Stanley Range. The results were major battles in New Guinea and the southern Solomon Islands.

On July 2, 1942, the Joint Chiefs ordered MacArthur to

capture the Japanese base at Rabaul, but first Guadalcanal and the airstrip the enemy was building had to be seized. This was to be undertaken by the navy and the 1st Marine Division. In conjunction, MacArthur was to occupy the Buna area on the north coast of Papua and build airstrips to support the Rabaul offensive. The Japanese attacked first at Buna and met only light resistance. Encouraged, they next went over the range toward Port Moresby. Meanwhile on August 7 the Marines landed at Guadalcanal and took the airfield. Not willing to give up this important piece of real estate, the Japanese countered by attacking the Americans with aircraft sent from Rabaul. Then one thousand Japanese soldiers came ashore at Guadalcanal after their navy had inflicted heavy losses on a combined U.S. and Australian fleet at Savo Island. The fighting at Guadalcanal turned into a battle of attrition until the Japanese withdrew in February 1943 after losing twenty-four thousand officers and men.

MacArthur's Australian forces faced similar challenges in Papua. The Japanese launched simultaneous attacks on August 26. One attack took place on the Kokoda Trail that meandered through the Owen Stanley Range; and in another, Japanese marines landed at Milne Bay. It took until September 6 before the Australians, with the help of reinforcements, outlasted the Japanese and they made no further attempts to resume the offensive.

The Australians soon defeated the Japanese at Milne Bay, but a series of defeats in the Kokoda Trail campaign had a depressing effect back in Australia. On August 30, MacArthur radioed Washington that unless action was taken, the New Guinea Force would be overwhelmed. Having committed all the available

Australian troops, MacArthur decided to send American troops. The 32nd Infantry Division, a poorly trained National Guard division, was selected to carry out a flanking maneuver.

A series of embarrassing American reverses in the Battle of Buna-Gona led to outspoken criticism of the American troops by Blamey and other Australians. MacArthur sent Lieutenant General Robert L. Eichelberger to "take Buna, or not come back alive." MacArthur moved the advanced echelon of GHQ to Port Moresby on November 6, 1942. Buna finally fell on January 3, 1943, and MacArthur awarded the Distinguished Service Cross to twelve officers for "precise execution of operations." In his order of January 9 announcing the DSC citations, MacArthur made it clear who was responsible for the recent success: "To almighty God I give thanks for that guidance which has brought us this success in our great Crusade. His is the honor, the power, and the glory forever, Amen."[3]

Once again the ugly nickname of "Dugout Doug" preyed up on MacArthur. Most recently he had been criticized for directing the Buna-Gona operation from Port Moresby and Brisbane, a mere forty-minute plane ride from the action. And again he proved that his detractors didn't know the real MacArthur. During the amphibious landings on the Admiralties, he arrived soon after his men and commenced to pace out an airstrip to determine its suitability, fully exposing himself to the enemy. Later during the fighting in Leyte he did the same thing and while in Luzon he came under fire inspecting frontline positions. His escort begged him to take cover, but MacArthur ignored his advice. "I'm not under fire," he said. "Those bullets are not intended for me."[4]

As MacArthur geared up for the next offensive he became increasingly dissatisfied with Brett and the Allied Air Forces as a whole. The two never really got along and in August 1942, MacArthur selected Major General George C. Kenney to replace Brett. Kenney's application of air power in support of Blamey's ground forces would soon prove critical to the Australian victory in the Battle of Wau. There was another change at the top as well. The following month Vice Admiral Arthur S. Carpender replaced Vice Admiral Leary as commander of Allied Naval Forces SWPA. Commonly referred to as "MacArthur's Navy," it consisted of only five cruisers, eight destroyers, twenty submarines, and seven small craft.

After the costly battle to take Buna, on the northern coast of Papua, MacArthur endorsed a plan to bypass the entrenched Japanese at Rabaul by utilizing superior air power and amphibious landings. Codenamed Operation Cartwheel, it was MacArthur's most brilliant operation of World War II. While combined Australian and U.S. forces advanced along the north coast of New Guinea, the Marines continued a trek through the Solomons to Bougainville.

In New Guinea, a country without roads, large-scale transportation of men and matériel would have to be accomplished by aircraft or ships. A multipronged approach was employed to solve this problem. Disassembled landing craft were shipped to Australia, where they were built in Cairns. The range of these small landing craft was to be greatly extended by the landing ships of Rear Admiral Daniel E. Barbey's VII Amphibious Force, which began arriving in late 1942. Barbey's force formed part of

Carpender's newly formed Seventh Fleet. Carpender reported to MacArthur as Supreme Allied Commander, SWPA, but to Admiral Ernest King as Commander Seventh Fleet, which was part of King's United States Fleet. Since the Seventh Fleet had no aircraft carriers, the range of naval operations SWPA was limited by that of the fighter aircraft of the Fifth Air Force. Although a few long-range P-38 Lightning fighters had arrived in SWPA in late 1942, further deliveries were suspended because of the demands of Operation Torch in North Africa.

Among those receiving the DSC was Eichelberger, who was miffed that some of the other recipients had not served the entire time at the front, but had merely visited for a short period. Nothing came of his complaint. For his part, MacArthur was awarded his third Distinguished Service Medal, and the Australian government made him an honorary Knight Grand Cross of the Order of the Bath.

Not wanting to lose the momentum, MacArthur sent Sutherland to meet with the Joint Chiefs of Staff at the Pacific Military Conference in March 1943. There he presented the plan for Operation Cartwheel and it was approved. Cartwheel would be an advance on Rabaul, but with a lack of resources, particularly heavy bomber aircraft, MacArthur had to delay the final stage of the plan, the capture of Rabaul itself, until 1944. MacArthur explained his strategy:

> My strategic conception for the Pacific Theater, which I out-
> lined after the Papuan Campaign and have since consistently
> advocated, contemplates massive strikes against only main

strategic objectives, utilizing surprise and air-ground striking power supported and assisted by the fleet. This is the very opposite of what is termed "island hopping" which is the gradual pushing back of the enemy by direct frontal pressure with the consequent heavy casualties which will certainly be involved. Key points must of course be taken but a wise choice of such will obviate the need for storming the mass of islands now in enemy possession. "Island hopping" with extravagant losses and slow progress . . . is not my idea of how to end the war as soon and as cheaply as possible. New conditions require for solution and new weapons require for maximum application new and imaginative methods. Wars are never won in the past.[5]

As the war in the Pacific slowly turned in favor of the Allies, largely because of MacArthur, his own government reached out to show its appreciation for him. General Marshall proposed the awarding of the Medal of Honor to the SWPA commander and President Roosevelt approved. It was announced on March 25, 1943, and the citation read in part: "For conspicuous leadership in preparing the Philippine Islands to resist conquest, for gallantry and intrepidity above and beyond the call of duty in action against invading Japanese forces . . . His calm judgment in each crisis, inspired his troops . . . and confirmed the faith of the American people in their armed forces." Rejected twice before, MacArthur now joined his father in receiving America's most distinguished medal. This was the first time the decoration had been bestowed upon both a father and his son.

★ ★ ★

The main offensive began with the landing at Lae by Major General George Wootten's Australian 9th Division and the 2nd Engineer Special Brigade on September 4, 1943. The next day MacArthur watched the landing at Nadzab by paratroops of the 503rd Parachute Infantry from a B-17 circling overhead. The B-17 made the trip on three engines because one failed soon after leaving Port Moresby, but MacArthur insisted that it fly on to Nadzab. MacArthur was awarded the Air Medal for this decision.

Major General George Alan Vasey's Australian 7th Division and Wooten's 9th Division converged on Lae, which fell on September 16. MacArthur advanced his timetable and ordered the 7th Division to capture Kaiapit and Dumpu, while the 9th Division mounted an amphibious assault on Finschhafen. Here, the offensive bogged down. Part of the problem was that MacArthur had based his decision to assault Finschhafen on Willoughby's intelligence assessment that only 350 Japanese defenders were there when in actuality there were nearly 5,000. A furious battle ensued until the Japanese were thrown off the Huon Peninsula town they had occupied since March 10, 1942.

In early November, MacArthur's plan for a westward advance along the coast of New Guinea to the Philippines was incorporated into plans for the war against Japan approved at the Cairo Conference. Three months later, airmen reported no signs of enemy activity in the Admiralty Islands. Although his intelligence staff did not agree that the islands had been evacuated, MacArthur ordered an amphibious landing on Los Negros Island, marking the beginning of the Admiralty Islands campaign. MacArthur accompanied the assault force aboard USS *Phoenix*, the flagship of Vice Admiral Thomas C. Kinkaid, who had recently replaced Carpender as commander of the Seventh Fleet. MacArthur, who came ashore with Kinkaid only seven hours after the first wave of landing craft, was awarded the Bronze Star for his actions in this campaign. After six weeks of fierce fighting, the 1st Cavalry Division captured the islands; the campaign officially ended on May 18, 1944.

In a brilliant move, MacArthur bypassed the Japanese forces at Hansa Bay and Wewak and assaulted Hollandia and Aitape, which Willoughby reported to be lightly defended. Kenney's new P-39s destroyed hundreds of enemy plans around Hollandia. They were supported by the aircraft carriers of the Pacific Fleet. Though risky, the operation turned out to be a brilliant success. MacArthur caught the Japanese off guard and cut off Lieutenant General Hatazo Adachi's Japanese XVIII Army in the Wewak area. Because the Japanese were not expecting an attack, the garrison was weak and Allied casualties were relatively light. The terrain turned out to be less suitable for airbase development than first thought, however, forcing MacArthur to seek better locations farther west. Moreover, while bypassing Japanese forces had great tactical merit, it had the serious strategic drawback of tying up large numbers of Allied troops in order to contain them, and Adachi was far from beaten.

MacArthur and a group of U.S. Army and Philippine officers wade ashore at Leyte Island, Philippines Islands (1944).

MacArthur greets Emperor Hirohito at the U.S. Embassy in Tokyo (1945).

MacArthur at his desk in the State, War and Navy Building when he was chief of staff (1944).

Douglas and Jean MacArthur standing beside his aircraft the *Bataan*.

FIFTEEN

Return to the Philippines

MACARTHUR WAS ANXIOUS to commence the long awaited return to the Philippines, but it would take convincing the joint chiefs and the president that this was the right direction for the Pacific Theater. Marshall summoned MacArthur to meet with President Roosevelt in Hawaii on July 26, 1944. The exact reason for the meeting was not told to MacArthur, but it was likely to discuss the next phase of action against the Japanese. Admirals Nimitz and Leahy were also in attendance. MacArthur was less than excited about going. Roosevelt was not his favorite person and since the president was in the midst of a reelection campaign, the general felt it was one big photo opportunity to distort how well the commander in chief and the SWPA commander got along.

Also, MacArthur was appalled at the idea of leaving his command in the middle of a war. Aboard the B-17 that took him to Oahu, he paced up and down the aisle grumbling to anyone who would listen: "In the First World War I never for a moment left my division, even when wounded by gas and ordered to the hospital. In all my fighting days I never before had to turn my back on my assignment."[1] Roosevelt impatiently waited on board the *Baltimore* for MacArthur. The others were already there when all of a sudden the noise of a piercing siren got louder and louder. Approaching the dock at Pearl Harbor was a motorcycle escort followed by what one observer called "the longest open car I have ever seen."[2]

MacArthur, in the back seat wearing his now trademark leather flying jacket and battered khaki field marshal's cap, waved to the crowd who had gathered to see what all of the commotion was about. Traveling alone, MacArthur walked up the gangplank and stopped midway to acknowledge the thunderous cheers, then went below deck to greet an astonished Roosevelt. The president responded: "Hello Douglas, what are you doing with that leather jacket on?" MacArthur replied that he had just flown in from Australia and "it's pretty cold up there."[3]

Much to MacArthur's annoyance, the following day Leahy, Nimitz, and he accompanied Roosevelt to inspect various military installations around Oahu. Roosevelt, to his credit, attempted to make MacArthur comfortable. The president did most of the talking. He discussed the previous World War and when they had worked together even before that. Not until after dinner that evening did the group get down to business. Roosevelt pointed at a large map of the Pacific and asked: "Well, Douglas, where do we go from here?" MacArthur confidently responded, "Leyte, Mr. President, and then Luzon." He explained that liberating the Philippines next was the moral thing to do. He had made a promise to the Filipino people and the troops left behind that he would be back for them. Roosevelt and Leahy were on his side, but Nimitz was not.

Admiral Nimitz wanted to bypass the Philippines and invade Formosa, a more direct route for a final assault on Japan's home islands. Although the issue was not settled, when the meeting ended, both Roosevelt and Leahy were convinced of the soundness of MacArthur's plan. In September, Halsey's carriers made a series of air strikes on the Philippines. As a result, the decision was made to invade Mindanao, the southernmost island by the end of the year, but it was moved up when Admiral Halsey's bombers reported light opposition in the central Philippines. The Joint Chiefs then decided to bypass Mindanao and invade Leyte in October. MacArthur's moment of glory was about to take place.

At a few minutes after ten o'clock on the morning of October 20, 1944, the first soldiers of MacArthur's liberation force landed on Leyte. Following four hours of heavy naval gunfire, Sixth Army forces landed on assigned beaches that afternoon. Troops from X Corps pushed across a four-mile stretch of beach between Tacloban Airfield and the Palo River. Fifteen miles to the south, XXIV Corps units came ashore across a three-mile beach between San José and the Daguitan River.

Prior to the operation to retake the Philippines, Lieutenant Courtney Whitney joined the staff of SWPA at the urging of

Sutherland. He had served in World War I as a pursuit pilot and then worked as a corporate lawyer in Manila before returning to the United States. In 1940 he returned to active duty and served as an intelligence officer with the Fourteenth Air Force in China when MacArthur summoned him. Whitney was given responsibility for Philippine civil affairs. According to William Manchester,

> from the standpoint of the guerrillas he was a disastrous choice. Undiplomatic and belligerent, he was condescending toward all Filipinos, except those who, like himself, had substantial investments in the Philippines . . . and by the time MacArthur was ready to land on Leyte, Whitney had converted most of the staff to reactionaryism. At his urging the General barred OSS agents from the Southwest Pacific, because Whitney suspected they would aid leftwing guerrillas.[4]

MacArthur's triumphant return to the Philippines was the largest amphibious operation mounted by American and Allied forces to date in the Pacific Theater. He was designated as supreme commander of sea, air, and land forces drawn from both the Southwest and Central Pacific theaters of operation. Allied naval and air support forces consisted primarily of the U.S. Seventh Fleet under Vice Admiral Thomas C. Kinkaid. With 701 ships, including 127 warships, Kinkaid's fleet would transport and put ashore the landing force. The Royal Australian Navy forces and its three landing ships and five auxiliary vessels assisted them.

The U.S. Sixth Army under Lieutenant General Walter Krueger, with two corps of two divisions each, was the main combat force. Organizing the beachhead, supplying units ashore, and constructing or improving roads and airfields was tasked to the newly organized Sixth Army Service Command under Major General Hugh J. Casey. In all, Krueger had 202,500 ground troops under his command. On Leyte, about 3,000 Filipino guerrillas under Lieutenant Colonel Ruperto Kangleon awaited the landing forces.

As Krueger's forces landed on the beaches of Leyte on October 20, MacArthur watched the action from the USS *Nashville*. From his vantage point he could see that the army was not advancing very far; snipers were still active and the area was under sporadic mortar fire. At 1:00 p.m. he boarded a LCM (landing craft, medium). The landing craft was ten miles from the shore and the trip took ninety minutes. At 2:30 MacArthur grew impatient and ordered the ramp lowered, stepped knee deep into the water, and strode toward the beach followed by Philippine president Sergio Osmeña and others in the entourage. Both MacArthur and the president gave radio broadcasts, but MacArthur's was the more memorable. It rivaled the one he had given in Brisbane two years before.

> People of the Philippines: I have returned. By the grace of Almighty God our forces stand again on Philippine soil—soil consecrated in the blood of our two peoples. We have come dedicated and committed to the task of destroying every vestige of enemy control over your daily lives, and of restoring upon a foundation of indestructible strength, the liberties of your people.[5]

A photograph was taken by a U.S. Army Signal Corps photographer as MacArthur and members of his staff and entourage waded ashore. This photo is arguably one of the most famous from World War II, showing MacArthur striding confidently through the surf toward the beach, looking like the epitome of a resolute leader. His facial expression may have had more to do with irritation over the situation than the historic import of the occasion. It is rumored that MacArthur was so pleased with the photo that he reenacted the event to try to improve it. There is no proof this ever happened.

Adverse weather and valiant Japanese resistance continued to slow the American advance ashore. MacArthur asked Nimitz for carriers to support the Sixth Army, but they proved to be no substitute for land-based aircraft, and the lack of air cover permitted the Japanese army to pour troops into Leyte. By the end of December, Krueger's headquarters estimated that five thousand Japanese remained on Leyte. At the end of December MacArthur considered the campaign over, except for some minor mopping up.

Eichelberger's Eighth Army would kill more than twenty-seven thousand Japanese on Leyte between then and the end of the campaign in May 1945. On December 18, 1944, MacArthur was promoted to the new five-star rank of General of the Army—one day before Nimitz was promoted to Fleet Admiral, also a five-star rank. To show his appreciation for the Allied effort thus far, MacArthur had a Filipino silversmith make the rank badges from American, Australian, Dutch, and Filipino coins.

Next, MacArthur ordered an invasion of Mindoro, where there were good potential airfield sites around the San Jose area.

Willoughby estimated, this time correctly, that the island had only about one thousand Japanese defenders. The problem was getting there. A parachute drop was considered, but the airfields on Leyte lacked the space to hold the required transport aircraft. The navy balked at sending escort carriers into the restricted waters of the Sulu Sea, and the air command could not guarantee land-based air cover. It was going to be a hazardous operation and MacArthur's staff talked him out of accompanying the invasion on the *Nashville*. When the invasion force entered the Sulu Sea, a kamikaze struck the ship, killing 133 people and wounding 190 more, including the task force commander, Brigadier General William C. Dunkel. The landings were made unopposed on December 15, 1944, and within two weeks Australian and American engineers had three airstrips in operation.

Willoughby's next intelligence reports were not so accurate. He estimated the strength of General Tomoyuki Yamashita's forces on Luzon at 137,000, while Sixth Army's intelligence estimated it at 234,000. Sixth Army Brigadier General Clyde D. Eddleman attempted to lay out the reasons for the Sixth Army's assessment, but MacArthur's response was "Bunk!" He believed that Willoughby's estimate was too high. In actuality, all the estimates were too low: Yamashita had more than 287,000 troops on Luzon. This time MacArthur traveled on the USS *Boise*, watching as the ship was near-missed by a bomb and torpedoes fired by midget submarines. Later that day MacArthur issued a communiqué that read: "The decisive battle for the liberation of the Philippines and the control of the Southwest Pacific is at hand. General MacArthur is in personal command at the front and landed with his assault troops."[6]

MacArthur now focused on the capture of the Port of Manila and the airbase at Clark Field, which were required to support future operations. He urged his frontline commanders on. On January 25, 1945, he moved his advance headquarters forward to Hacienda Luisita, closer to the front than Krueger's at Calasiao. On January 30, MacArthur ordered the 1st Cavalry Division's commander, Major General Verne D. Mudge, to conduct a rapid advance on Manila. On February 3, it reached the northern outskirts of Manila and the campus of the University of Santo Tomas where thirty-seven hundred internees were liberated.

Unknown to the Americans, Rear Admiral Sanji Iwabuchi had decided to defend Manila to the death. The Battle of Manila raged for the next three weeks. In order to spare the civilian population, MacArthur prohibited the use of air strikes, but thousands of civilians died in the crossfire of Japanese massacres. He also refused to restrict the traffic of civilians who clogged the roads in and out of Manila, placing humanitarian concerns above military ones except for emergencies.

The destruction of the Manila Hotel was disheartening to MacArthur. He reached it on February 22, but it was too late. The building was on fire, including the penthouse suite that had been the scene of so many memories. Gone was MacArthur's eight-thousand-volume military library, which included books he had inherited from his father. But in the end Manila was under American control and for his part in the operation, MacArthur was awarded his third Distinguished Service Cross.

Although MacArthur had no specific directive from the Joint Chiefs to do so, and the fighting on Luzon was far from over, he committed the Eighth Army, Seventh Fleet, and Thirteenth Air Force to a series of operations to liberate the remainder of the Philippines from the Japanese. A series of fifty-two amphibious landings was made in the central and southern Philippines between February and July 1945. In the GHQ communiqué on July 5, MacArthur announced that the Philippines had now been liberated and all operations ended, although Yamashita still held out in northern Luzon.

Starting in May 1945, MacArthur used his Australian troops in the invasion of Borneo. MacArthur accompanied the assault on Labuan on the USS *Boise* and visited the troops ashore, along with Lieutenant General Sir Leslie Morshead and Air Vice Marshal William Bostock. En route back to his headquarters in Manila, he visited Davao, where he told Eichelberger that no more than four thousand Japanese remained alive on Mindanao. A few months later, six times that number would surrender. In July 1945, he set out on the *Boise* once more to be with the Australian 7th Division for the landing at Balikpapan. MacArthur was awarded his fourth Distinguished Service Medal.

In April 1945, MacArthur was named commander in chief U.S. Army Forces Pacific (AFPAC), in charge of all army and army air force units in the Pacific, except the Twentieth Air Force. At the same time, Nimitz became commander of all naval forces. Command in the Pacific remained divided. GHQ became AFPAC headquarters in addition to SWPA. This reorganization, which took some months to actually accomplish, was part of the preparations for Operation Downfall, the invasion of Japan.

The first phase, the invasion of Kyushu, known as Operation

Olympic, was scheduled to commence on November 1, 1945, and MacArthur would lead the ground forces. A ground attack, he believed, was the only way the Japanese homeland could be defeated. Although air bombardments would be less costly in casualties, there was no guarantee of their effectiveness as shown in the European Theater when intensive bombing there failed to force Germany to surrender.[7] Also in April President Roosevelt died and his vice president, Harry S. Truman, took over as commander in chief. Strangely, MacArthur made no mention of the president's death in *Reminiscences*. Even with so much animosity between them, Roosevelt's death must have impacted MacArthur in some way.

Although he directed his staff to begin planning for the invasion of Japan, and was hopeful about *Olympic*, MacArthur never believed there was going to be an invasion. He thought the Japanese could be defeated by attrition, but at the end of July he learned they were going to be beaten in another way. MacArthur was briefed about the Manhattan Project and the development of the atomic bomb. He was now certain the war would be over within a matter of two weeks. He was correct; within days after the bombs were dropped on Hiroshima and Nagasaki, the Japanese gave up. The war may have ended but there was still plenty of work to do. President Truman named MacArthur Supreme Commander for the Allied Powers (SCAP). He would not only take the surrender but also oversee the occupation of Japan.

SIXTEEN

Occupation

WOULD THE FORMAL surrender take place at sea or on land? President Truman settled the debate quickly. He was from Missouri and the naval ship bearing his state's name was at sea south of Japan. He ordered the battleship USS *Missouri* to Tokyo Bay and the surrender ceremony was set for September 2. MacArthur, Nimitz, and Halsey would accept the surrender from the eleven-man Japanese delegation in front of Allied admirals, generals, correspondents, photographers, and other interested onlookers. Hovering over the battleship that day was the American flag that had flown above the United States Capitol on December 7, 1941.

Before the surrender document was signed, MacArthur addressed the crowd and, as usual, his speech was eloquent and fitting.

The issues, involving divergent ideals and ideologies, have been determined on the battlefields of the world and hence are not for our discussions or debate. Nor is it for us here to meet, representing as we do a majority of the people of the earth, in a spirit of distrust, malice or hatred. But rather it is for us both victors and vanquished, to rise to that higher dignity which alone befits the sacred purposes we are about to serve, committing all our people unreservedly to faithful compliance.[1]

MacArthur recalled that he had received no instructions on what to say or do that day. "I was on my own," he said, "standing on the quarterdeck with only God and my own conscience to guide me." His words were a great relief to the Japanese delegation and set the tone for how MacArthur would govern the occupation of their country. After he spoke, the Japanese and Allies signed the document and then the greatest flyover in history, four hundred B-29s and thirty-five hundred carrier planes, interrupted the solemn occasion. As the Japanese slowly departed the *Missouri*, MacArthur entered another room aboard the ship and said a few final thoughts that weren't intended for their ears: "Today the guns are silent . . . A great tragedy has ended. A great victory has been won."[2]

General Wainwright was among those witnessing the surrender aboard the *Missouri*. On the evening of August 3, 1945, MacArthur and Wainwright saw each other for the first time in more than three years. That afternoon a plane carrying Wainwright and other released prisoners landed at Yokohama, Japan. Wainwright's limousine led a motorcade to the New Grand

Hotel, while Japanese onlookers bowed in respect. MacArthur was at dinner when Wainwright's party entered the main dining room. Those present—mostly Americans—fell silent, all eyes on Wainwright. MacArthur was shocked by his appearance and by the fact that he could walk only with a cane. "His eyes were sunken," MacArthur remembered. "His hair was white and his skin looked like old shoe leather."[3]

MacArthur rose, strode over to Wainwright, and the two old soldiers embraced. Both men seemed close to tears. They sat down to dinner, and Wainwright told a little of his three years as a prisoner. He spoke of the humiliation of the surrender and of his fear that his military career was over. MacArthur sought to ease his mind, asking what assignment he would like. Wainwright asked to command a corps under MacArthur. "Why Jim," he replied "you can have a corps with me any time you want it." But Wainwright would never again serve under MacArthur.

With the fighting behind him, MacArthur now fixated on rebuilding the Japanese government so its leaders and the people of Japan could move forward. There were two main objectives before him: end militarism, democratize the country, and remove and repair its economy. Essential to the success of a new Japan was replacement of the old constitution. The one now in place, the Meiji Constitution, was written in 1889, and named after the emperor Meiji—the grandfather of the then-reigning emperor, Hirohito. The parliamentary government, or Diet, came under the emperor. Members of the Diet were both appointed from wealthy families and elected by male voters who paid high taxes. Since a small number of Japanese owned land or had wealth, few people participated in the government prior to World War II. A feudal system existed in Japan before 1945. Land was leased and not owned by farmers, women had no rights over property and marriage, voting rights belonged to the wealthy few, and there was little freedom of the press.

Building on many of the aspects of the United States Constitution, MacArthur and a small staff drew up a new document for Japan. The elements found in the new Japanese constitution include a Bill of Rights, equal rights, freedom of religion, political parties, abolishment of war, abolishment of feudalism, government power residing in the people not the emperor, free enterprise, freedom of speech, right of minimum standard of living, right to unions or collective bargaining, and an end to discrimination of women, religion, races.

One important change listed above specifically gave governmental power to the people. The Meiji constitution explicitly stated that the emperor held supreme power over Japan because as a descendant of the sun goddess, the emperor Hirohito was semi-divine. To encourage democracy, it was important that the Japanese people believed that all humans, including the emperor, had equal status under the law. Following MacArthur's instructions, Hirohito addressed the Japanese people and denounced his semi-divinity.

On September 6, 1945, President Truman approved a document titled "U.S. Initial Post-Surrender Policy for Japan." The document set two main objectives for the occupation: eliminate Japan's war potential and turn the country into a Western-style nation with pro-American orientation. MacArthur believed his first priority was to set up a food distribution network. Following the collapse of the ruling government and the wholesale destruction of most major cities, virtually everyone was starving.

The United States government encouraged democratic reform in Japan and sent billions of dollars in aid, but many in Congress were against feeding the enemy. MacArthur ignored them, arguing that riots would take place unless food was brought in. Food that had been set aside for the invasion of Japan was sent to Tokyo. Even with these measures, millions of people were still on the brink of starvation for several years after the surrender. When MacArthur arrived, Tokyo was a virtual wasteland because of the firebombs during the war. One could almost see clear across the city.

Once the food network was in place, MacArthur set out to win the support of Hirohito. The two men met for the first time on September 27; the photograph of them is one of the most famous in Japanese history. Many were shocked, however, that MacArthur wore his standard duty uniform with no tie instead of his dress uniform when meeting the emperor. MacArthur likely did this on purpose in order to send a message that he was in charge and the emperor answered to him.

While other reforms were taking place, various military tribunals, most notably the International Military Tribunal for the Far East in Ichigaya, were trying Japan's war criminals and sentencing many low-level officers to death and imprisonment. General MacArthur gave many others, such as the imperial family, immunity from criminal prosecution. Two of Japan's most ruthless generals were convicted and executed. Masaharu Homma was convicted on suspect evidence that he orchestrated the death march that followed the surrender of Bataan, and Tomoyuki Yamashita was charged for atrocities committed by Japanese troops in Manila. Most Americans were concerned with the war tribunals taking place in Germany and paid little attention to what was going on in Japan.

MacArthur ordered the Japanese to disarm its troops. In the weeks following the surrender, millions of soldiers returned to their homeland from China and other parts of the Japanese empire and turned in their guns and uniforms. At this point Japan ceased to have an army. Its secret police force was abolished and political prisoners were freed. In March 1946 the new constitution was adopted by Japan's legislature. Included in the constitution was a no-war provision, insisted upon by MacArthur. Much controversy arose from this, but it made sense. He was not denying Japan the right to defend itself; Japan simply was not allowed to make war beyond its shores.

The following month saw a high turnout for the election of a new legislature. Women took 38 out of 466 seats. They helped push through new reforms that revised marriage and divorce laws so that wives were no longer the "property" of their husbands.

Much was accomplished during the first phase of the U.S. occupation. Significant democratic reforms such as votes for women, legalization of trade unions, and anti-feudal land reform were introduced. One of the more radical reforms MacArthur initiated was the establishment of a censorship bureaucracy that "extended into every aspect of public expression." During the occupation, U.S. censors checked 330 million pieces of mail and monitored 800,000 private phone conversations. Newspapers, books, public broadcasting, and cinema were heavily censored. In Tokyo a stage show in which one of the cast sang, "How can we have democracy with two emperors?" mocking Hirohito and MacArthur, was banned.

MacArthur wanted an upbeat, positive outlook and subjects such as criticism of the United States, criticism of the emperor, food shortages, the black market, warnings about World War III, fraternization, and references to censorship were discouraged. While the attacks on Hiroshima and Nagasaki were not officially on the list of forbidden subjects, eyewitness accounts and other reports were suppressed.

MacArthur was known to keep unusual office hours. Typically he would arrive just before 11:00 a.m., leave at 2:30, and then come back around 5:00 or 5:30 and stay until 8:30 or 9:00 p.m. It was not unheard of for him to stay until midnight. A lifelong friend, General Robert Wood, once confronted MacArthur about his peculiar schedule: "Douglas, I hear you keep atrocious work hours. You've got to stop that." MacArthur moved slightly and in a blunt tone responded: "Well Bob, I like them." Wood never brought up the subject again. The Japanese people revered MacArthur and followed him wherever he went. Thousands wrote him letters and he reportedly read each one and, with the help of his staff and translators, replied to all of them.

As 1948 approached, the United States was about to undertake another presidential election. Opinion polls showed most Americans were not high on Truman and once again MacArthur was mentioned as the Republican candidate. This time he approved and "MacArthur for president" committees were set up in early primary states. While the more conservative and anti-Communist wings of the Republican Party favored him, there was stronger isolationist movement within the party and he lost most of the primaries. Among them was Wisconsin, which MacArthur declared as his home state. Thus ended MacArthur's bid to become commander in chief.

Despite his heavy workload, MacArthur found time for Jean and Arthur and, as before, he doted heavily on his son. Some of his father's colleagues described Arthur as "delicate, sweet, lively, frail, gentle, sensitive, and sweet."[4] He later adopted his father's interest in music and the theater, but did not continue the MacArthur military tradition. Douglas had great expectations for Arthur and sometime during the war he wrote the following, entitled "A Father's Prayer."

> Build me a son, O Lord, who will be strong enough to know when he is weak, and brave enough to face himself when he is afraid; one who will be proud and unbending in honest defeat, and humble and gentle in victory.
>
> Build me a son whose wishes will not take the place of deeds: a son who will know Thee—and that to know himself is the foundation stone of knowledge.
>
> Lead him, I pray, not in the path of ease and comfort, but under the stress and spur of difficulties and challenge. Here let him learn to stand up in the storm: here let him learn compassion for those who fail.
>
> Build me a son whose heart will be clear, whose goal will be high; a son who will master himself before he seeks to

master other men; one who will reach into the future, yet never forget the past.[5]

And after all these things are his, add, I pray, enough of a sense of humor, so that he may always be serious, yet never take himself too seriously. Give him humility, so that he may always remember the simplicity of true greatness, the open mind of true wisdom, and the meekness of true strength.[6]

As the current decade came to a close, so did peace. Hostility between the United States and the Soviet Union was intense, mostly over an arms race to see who could build more atomic bombs. It was a cold war and no shots were fired. China was also flexing its muscle and the country was in the midst of civil war between the Communists and the Nationalists. Back in the United States anti-Communist hysteria was on the rise, and a senator from Wisconsin, Joseph McCarthy, did much to fuel such sentiment. Meanwhile, MacArthur watched carefully as another part of Asia was about to come apart—Korea.

MacArthur addresses members of Congress after his removal as UN commander during the Korean War (1951).

MacArthur and Eighth Army commander Lieutenant General Mathew B. Ridgeway leaving the 35th Infantry Regiment headquarters during the Korean War (1951).

MacArthur signs surrender document aboard the USS Missouri. Standing directly behind him is Lt. General Jonathan Wainwright (1945).

MacArthur, President Franklin D. Roosevelt and Admiral Chester Nimitz aboard a cruiser of the U.S. Pacific Fleet in Pearl Harbor (1944).

MacArthur and President Harry S. Truman meet for the first time on Wake Island during the Korean War (1950).

SEVENTEEN

The Korean War

MACARTHUR WAS ASLEEP in his bedroom at the U.S. Embassy in Tokyo when the telephone rang during the early morning hours of Sunday, June 25, 1950. On the other end was the duty officer at headquarters with startling news: the North Koreans had just stormed across the 38th parallel and attacked South Korea. It was five o'clock and a groggy MacArthur first thought he was dreaming, probably having a nightmare about a similar early Sunday call on December 7, 1941, when he was asleep in his penthouse at the Manila Hotel. Then reality sunk in. His chief of staff Almond entered the room moments later and asked: "Any orders, General?"[1]

Korea had been a Japanese possession since 1910. Following the defeat of Japan in 1945, Soviet troops occupied Korea north of the 38th line of latitude (usually referred to as the 38th parallel). American troops occupied the area south of this line. By agreement, Soviet and American forces withdrew from Korea in 1948 and it was then separated into two countries. North Korea, which bordered China, had become a Communist state heavily armed by the Soviet Union, while South Korea maintained close ties with the United States. In 1949, the Chinese Civil War ended. Victorious Chinese Communist forces drove the anti-Communist Nationalist Chinese off the China mainland to the island of Formosa (now called Taiwan).

President Truman's containment policy sought to stop Communist aggression, especially against Europe and Japan, but his administration officials made confusing public statements that seemed to exclude Formosa and Korea as areas to be defended by the United States. With that said, North Korea was apparently encouraged by the United States policy and believed it could attack the southern part of the country without suffering any consequences. Their main ally, the Soviet Union, also believed the chances of intervention were slim, and approved a military action by North Korea. Since January 1950 the Soviets had boycotted United Nations Security Council meetings over protest that Nationalist China was allowed membership, but Communist China had been denied a seat. They believed the UN to be weak and unthreatening.

North Korea also had other reasons to feel confident. Under the leadership of Kim Il Sung, the country had built an army of 135,000 troops; a vast majority were skilled fighters who had served in China and the Soviet Union during World War II. He had eight full divisions, each including a regiment of artillery; two divisions at half strength; two separate regiments; and an armored brigade equipped with Soviet T34 medium tanks. Along with the ground forces were 180 Soviet fighters and attack bombers and a few naval patrol crafts. On the other hand, the Republic of Korea (ROK) forces in the south were comprised of just 95,000 troops. It also had eight divisions, but only half were at full strength. There were no tanks, a handful of artillery howitzers, and a few planes. Most of its equipment had been acquired from the United States after World War II, and much of that was in poor condition. The Korean War was an offshoot of the Cold War. No one really saw it coming in the same sense as with the First and Second World Wars. Despite the fact that President Truman called it a "police action," it was a war in every sense of the definition. The United States, as the most influential body in the United Nations, took the lead in committing troops, armaments, and most of all, the strategy to try and bring the conflict to a swift conclusion.

Despite promises of matériel assistance from the U.S. Congress, it was slow in coming and as a result the South Koreans were crushed on June 25 and could do little but watch the North Koreans move down the west side of the peninsula toward the capital of Seoul. The city was reached three days later and the meager ROK troops trying to defend it were driven out, leaving more of their equipment behind. After briefly halting, the North Koreans continued across the Han River uncontested.

Early on the twenty-fifth, at the urging of the United States, an emergency meeting of the UN Security Council convened and adopted a resolution calling for the cessation of hostilities and the immediate withdrawal of North Korean forces to the 38th parallel. That night President Truman took matters into his own hands and ordered MacArthur to supply ROK forces with ammunition and equipment, evacuate Americans living in Korea who were in harm's way, and survey the peninsula for other ways to assist the South Koreans further. Assisting him in this endeavor was the U.S. Navy Seventh Fleet, which was now at Taiwan as a buffer between Chinese Nationalists and Communists.

MacArthur sprang into action. He deployed the transportation planes Truman requested and safely removed two thousand Americans and UN personnel. Then at the president's urging he gathered his forces that were part of the recently formed Far East Command (FEC). MacArthur did not have much to work with. Available to him were the 1st Cavalry Division and the 7th, 24th, and 25th Infantry divisions, which were the nucleus of the Eighth Army, and a small air force that was better prepared for defensive strategy than for offensive capability. On July 3 Truman named MacArthur commander of all military forces assisting the ROK and the general established the United Nations Command (UNC) and was given permission to commit ground forces. He led the UNC from Japan, but traveled to South Korea often to meet with the ground commanders.

With the North Koreans already across the Han, the best MacArthur could do at this point was to deploy his units piecemeal in a defensive posture to prevent further enemy advances and buy time before a larger force could be built up. On July 5, Task Force Smith, which consisted of 540 men, tried to head off the North Koreans near Suwon, south of Seoul. But they were attacked first in a heavy rain and easily repulsed by the superior forces. Task Force Smith fled in a disorderly retreat with more than 150 casualties and the loss of all equipment except small arms. American morale plummeted.

MacArthur tried on three more occasions to commit small forces to cut off the enemy and each time the North Koreans were able to turn the American flanks. He then reorganized and placed Lieutenant General Walton Walker in command of the Eighth Army and at the request of the South Korean government, Walker also commanded the ROK. While his forces were buying time in Korea, MacArthur brought over more troops from Japan. He stripped the 7th Infantry Division and placed those troops in the 1st Cavalry and 25th Divisions and they were ready to fight in the battle for Taejon on July 18. After two days of combat, the North Koreans surrounded the city, trapping the 24th Division before it managed to escape without its commander, Major General William F. Dean. He spent the next three years as a prisoner of the North Koreans.

Continuing to push the defenders south, the North Koreans were also running into trouble. The United States had brought over more planes and the Far East Air Force (FEAF) established air superiority; the UNC naval warships crushed the small North Korean navy and placed a tight blockade on the Korean coast. More importantly, North Korean supply lines grew thin. Still the North Koreans split their forces with the objective of Pusan in mind and continued to batter the opposition along the way. By the end of July, American casualties were more than six thousand and the South Koreans had lost nearly seventy thousand.

Desperately, in August, Walker ordered a stand along a

140-mile line that arched from the Korean Strait to the Sea of Japan, west and north of Pusan. He was supported by the South Koreans whose military advisers had reorganized them into two corps headquarters and five divisions. Walker spread his forces in a thin line and used his interior lines of communication to support the area where North Korean pressure was the greatest. Their forces had grown to thirteen divisions, but most of the new troops were inexperienced. Meanwhile, the Eighth Army was also increasing. MacArthur had convinced Truman to send more men and supplies to Korea. By September Walker had received five hundred medium tanks and the 5th Regimental Combat Team from Hawaii, and the 2nd Infantry Division and 1st Provisional Marine Brigade from the United States. Great Britain also sent over a brigade from Hong Kong. Walker's army was now holding on.

Meanwhile, MacArthur was developing a plan to deal a crushing blow on the North Korean forces. At the beginning of the war he recognized that the deeper they drove, the more vulnerable they would become. He could envelop them in a great amphibious assault, and he suggested the port at Inchon on the Yellow Sea as the landing site. It was about twenty-five miles east of Seoul, where Korea's main rail lines and roads converged. An amphibious force landing at Inchon would then have to move only a short distance to cut North Korea's supply lines and recapture the capital city. To make the operation successful MacArthur needed the Eighth Army to advance northward and cut off the enemy or force them to make a slow and difficult withdrawal through the mountains farther to the east.

To meet the troop strength for the operation he formed the

two-division X Corps and named his chief of staff, Almond, as corps commander. The corps consisted of the 7th Division, which would be augmented by eighty-six hundred South Korean recruits, and most of the 1st Marine Division that arrived from the United States. But before the operation could take place MacArthur needed approval from the Joint Chiefs of Staff and the navy, and neither were on board. The navy was concerned about the extreme Yellow Sea tides, which range as much as thirty feet, and the narrow channel approaches to Inchon as major risks to shipping. The Marines were worried about landing in the middle of a built-up area and having to scale high sea walls to reach the shore. Then there was the apprehension that Inchon would be heavily defended and losses could be heavy with no prospects of reinforcements any time soon. MacArthur was willing to take the gamble.

Inchon turned out perfectly and was one of MacArthur's greatest achievements during his long military career. On September 15 the X Corps came ashore against light resistance and although it soon stiffened, they swept inland during the next two weeks. The X Corps split with one part heading south and seizing Suwon and the other fighting its way through Seoul. The Marines did their part by using scaling ladders to storm ashore and fought off the minimal resistance that stood in the way.

MacArthur came ashore two days later and one of his first acts was to visit Colonel Lewis "Chesty" Puller, the famed commander of the 1st Marine Regiment. A witness to the event, company commander Major Edwin Simmons, later brigadier general, said MacArthur "completely dominated the scene" with his "crushed hat, sunglasses, leather jacket, and faded but carefully pressed khaki trousers."[2] On September 29, MacArthur, with President Syngman Rhee in tow, entered Seoul triumphantly. And just as MacArthur planned, Walker's Eighth Army attacked out of the Pusan perimeter and forced about thirty thousand of the North Korean forces to scatter through the mountains and escape across the 38th parallel. Several thousand more stayed behind to fight as guerillas in the mountains of South Korea. Suddenly the momentum of the war had shifted in favor of the UN forces.

Over the weekend of October 15 to 17, President Truman flew to Wake Island in the Pacific to meet General MacArthur for the first time. The most important question Truman asked MacArthur was whether he thought China would enter the war. The general confidently replied that the Chinese would not enter the fighting and the war would be over by Christmas. He could not have been more wrong. On November 25, 1950, nearly two hundred thousand Chinese soldiers poured across the Yalu River, forcing UN forces into a full retreat to the south. MacArthur demanded permission to bomb Chinese bases north of the Yalu in China itself. But Truman feared that if he allowed MacArthur such latitude the war might widen to include the Soviet Union, so the president and his advisers refused the request. Instead, they ordered him to organize a phased and orderly retreat. On December 29, Truman administration officials informed MacArthur that the United States had abandoned the goal of reunifying Korea.

MacArthur was infuriated at what he considered the Truman administration's sellout of Korea and proposed his own plan for victory. He called for a complete blockade of the Communist Chinese coastline and the bombing of industrial sites and other strategic targets within China. MacArthur also wanted to bring Nationalist Chinese troops from Formosa to fight in Korea. He went public to argue for his plan and this caused further consternation between him and Truman. MacArthur criticized the "politicians in Washington" for refusing to allow him to bomb Chinese bases north of the Yalu River. He did all this in spite of an order from his superiors in Washington not to make any public statements on foreign or military policy without first getting approval from the Department of State or Defense. MacArthur was on a collision course with his commander in chief.

When the Chinese offensive stalled just south of the 38th parallel in the spring of 1951, Truman began to work on a peace proposal. He wanted to reestablish the original border between North and South Korea and remove all foreign troops from both countries. Shortly after he learned of Truman's proposal, MacArthur announced his own terms for ending the fighting. Without obtaining clearance from Washington, he made a public statement that taunted the Chinese for failing to conquer South Korea. MacArthur then threatened to attack China unless its military went back across the border.

MacArthur's announcement was interpreted as an ultimatum to China. It completely overshadowed Truman's diplomatic efforts to negotiate a cease-fire. America's allies began to wonder who was really in charge of U.S. foreign and defense policy. Was it the president or his general? Truman considered MacArthur's actions insubordinate. A few days later the issue turned from bad to worse. MacArthur's Republican Party supporters in Congress released a letter from him in which he declared, "There is no substitute for victory." Truman at this point was at the end of his tether and needed to make a change. He met for several days with his top advisers. They all agreed that MacArthur had to go because civilian authority always overruled the military.

A little more than ten months before, MacArthur had been awakened from a sound sleep to receive the shocking news that North Korea had just attacked its southern neighbor. Now, on April 11, 1951, his sleep was again interrupted. This time he was napping after lunch when his aide, Colonel Sidney Huff, brought him an urgent message. It was sent from Chairman of the Joint Chiefs of Staff Omar N. Bradley, and it read:

> You will turn over your commands, effective at once, to Lieutenant General Matthew B. Ridgway. You are authorized to have issued such orders as are necessary to complete desired travel to such place as you select. My reasons for your replacement will be made concurrently to you of the foregoing message.[3]

MacArthur turned to his wife and said, "Jeannie, we are going home." With just three simple sentences the illustrious military career of Douglas MacArthur had ended. That same day President Truman was much more wordy in his official statement explaining why he had relieved MacArthur:

> With deep regret I have concluded that General of the Army Douglas MacArthur is unable to give his wholehearted support to the policies of the United States Government and of the United Nations in matters pertaining to his official duties. In view of the

specific responsibilities imposed upon me by the Constitution of the United States and the added responsibility which has been entrusted to me by the United Nations, I have decided that I must make a change of command in the Far East. I have, therefore, relieved General MacArthur of his commands and have designated Lt. Gen. Matthew B. Ridgway as his successor.

Full and vigorous debate on matters of national policy is a vital element in the constitutional system of our free democracy. It is fundamental, however, that military commanders must be governed by the policies and directives issued to them in the manner provided by our laws and Constitution. In time of crisis, this consideration is particularly compelling.

General MacArthur's place in history as one of our greatest commanders is fully established. The Nation owes him a debt of gratitude for the distinguished and exceptional service which he has rendered his country in posts of great responsibility. For that reason I repeat my regret at the necessity for the action I feel compelled to take in his case.[4]

Word of MacArthur's firing spread quickly around the world. President Truman gave a disappointing radio address on the evening of April 11. Those who tuned in expected the president to explain his rationale for firing MacArthur, but instead, he talked about his administration's policies on the war. Afterward tens of thousands of letters flooded the White House mailbox, the majority overwhelmingly in favor of MacArthur. Senator Robert Taft, a prominent Republican from Ohio, told the *Chicago Tribune* there should be immediate impeachment proceedings against Truman. A

Gallup poll conducted on April 14 found that 66 percent of those surveyed disapproved of Truman's decision to remove MacArthur, while only 25 percent approved of the president's action. Truman remained in office for another year and MacArthur returned home a hero.

In Japan, the Diet passed a resolution of gratitude for MacArthur, and Emperor Hirohito visited him at the embassy in person, the first time an emperor had ever visited a foreigner with no standing. In tribute the *Mainichi* newspaper said:

> MacArthur's dismissal is the greatest shock since the end of the war. He dealt with the Japanese people not as a conqueror but a great reformer. He was a noble political missionary. What he gave us was not material aid and democratic reform alone, but a new way of life, the freedom and dignity of the individual. We shall continue to love and trust him as one of the Americans who best understood Japan's position.[5]

MacArthur left Japan on April 16 and that morning 250,000 Japanese lined the streets to say goodbye to their beloved general. Signs read: "We Love You, MacArthur," "With Deep Regret," "Sayonara," and "We are Grateful to the General." When the MacArthurs arrived in San Francisco on April 18, 1951, the city threw him a ticker-tape parade that was attended by hundreds of thousands of people. And when he finally made it to the East Coast, MacArthur received an even larger ticker-tape parade in New York City, on April 22, 1951. An estimated five million people lined the streets to get a glimpse of the Defiant Soldier. It was the largest parade ever held in the city up until that time.

An Old Soldier Fades Away

MACARTHUR LOVED GIVING speeches and he delivered his most famous one before Congress on April 19, 1951. He had spoken in front of Congress many times before, mostly in vain attempts to defend his beloved army when so many wanted to see it depleted of men, supplies, and equipment. But this time was different. It was the speech of a lifetime, a culmination of five decades as a public servant. He had just been humiliated for carrying out his convictions and he intended to have the last say in the matter.

Before a captive audience and television cameras, he spoke for about an hour and a half. He opined on Asia and how it was the future, despite its impoverished and war-torn condition. China was the real enemy, not the Soviet Union, he assured his attentive audience. The constant interruption of wild applause and the standing ovations by Republicans and Democrats alike was the reason his speech took so long. MacArthur complained about the lack of reinforcements and restrictions placed on his command. But the best was yet to come. He ended his glorious speech with perhaps the greatest rhetoric ever spoken on Capitol Hill:

> I am closing my fifty-two years of military service. When I joined the Army even before the turn of the century, it was the fulfillment of all my boyish hopes and dreams. The world has turned over many times since I took the oath on the Plain at West Point, and the hopes and dreams have long since vanished. But I still remember the refrain of one of the most popular barrack ballads of that day which proclaimed most proudly that "Old soldiers never die, they just fade away." And like the old soldier of that ballad, I now close my military career and just fade away—an old soldier who tried to do his duty as God gave him the light to see that duty. Goodbye.[1]

Amidst the applause there were shouts of, "No! No!" Tears flowed. Witnesses said there was not a dry eye in the house. Two weeks later, he was back before Congress to testify before hearings on the Korean War. This time MacArthur was not at his best. During three days of testimony, he tried to assert that the Joint Chiefs approved all his recommendations on how to fight the war but that it was the White House that stood in the way. His claims were countered by Bradley, who said that MacArthur's desire to make China the focus of the conflict "would involve us in the wrong war, at the wrong place, at the wrong time, and with the wrong enemy."[2] MacArthur seemed uncomfortable when responding and he came off as defensive.

With another election on the horizon, his name was again bandied about as the Republican candidate, but this time he had far fewer supporters than before and his chances to run as a serious candidate were slim. He still had name recognition, especially among conservatives, and during the summer of 1952 MacArthur was asked to give a keynote speech at the Republican convention in Chicago. Sadly, the speech fell flat and diminished any hope that he might receive his party's nomination for president. To his disappointment the honor went to his former aide, the very popular Dwight D. Eisenhower. Ike won handily that November. Just before Christmas the two former soldiers met to discuss how to end the Korean War. MacArthur presented Eisenhower and his assistant with a memo containing eight proposals that included a couple of far-fetched ideas, including the bombing of China and the dropping of nuclear waste across North Korea. Neither one was taken seriously by the president-elect.

Much later on MacArthur was called upon to advise another president. President John F. Kennedy met with the old general on more than one occasion, and often the conversation turned to the impending war in Vietnam. MacArthur urged the young president not to commit troops there, but to focus his energies domestically. How American history might have changed had Kennedy not been assassinated and MacArthur's advice heeded.

By now MacArthur was spending much of his time

entertaining guests in 37-B, his elaborate, ten-room apartment at the Waldorf Towers in New York. Reportedly, the owner of the Waldorf, Conrad Hilton, combined three apartments into one to accommodate MacArthur and only charged $450 a month rent.[3] The towers were attached to the Waldorf Astoria hotel and among the other notables who resided there at various times were the Duke and Duchess of Windsor, Cole Porter, and gangsters Benjamin "Bugsy" Siegel and Charles "Lucky" Luciano. Former president Herbert Hoover lived there at the same time as the MacArthurs but on a separate floor, and he socialized with them on occasion.

Located between Park and Lexington Avenues in upper Manhattan, the neighborhood was ideal for Douglas and Jean. They could walk to Saint Bartholomew's Episcopal Church where they were members of the congregation. And some of New York's best clothing stores were also close by. Jean, like her husband, was fashion conscious and accumulated quite a wardrobe of clothes, jewelry, and shoes. Douglas was often seen in the menswear department of Saks Fifth Avenue shopping for suits.[4]

MacArthur pursued his interest in sports by attending boxing matches and baseball and football games. As one would expect, he adored the army's sports teams and was great friends with the football coach, who wrote MacArthur each week with details of the previous Saturday's games. Living in New York also afforded him the opportunity to enjoy another passion—the theater. MacArthur especially liked musicals and his attendance always brought a rousing applause from other theatergoers as he walked down the aisle to his seat.[5]

MacArthur also served for a brief period as chairman of the board of the Remington-Rand Corporation, a major defense contractor later named Sperry Rand. This was easy work as he only went to the company headquarters about three or four mornings a week. It was located an hour outside of New York City and he took his time getting there, usually arriving around lunchtime. MacArthur's role was largely one of prestige and advising on international affairs.[6] He preferred not to travel much, but in July 1961, MacArthur returned to the Philippines for the fiftieth anniversary of the country's independence. It was also a chance for him to meet with the survivors of Bataan and Corregidor for the last time.

When MacArthur had reached his eightieth birthday the year before, publisher Henry Luce approached him about writing his memoirs. Luce paid him nine hundred thousand dollars for the rights to a book that was eventually titled *Reminiscences*. It took MacArthur until the end of his life to finish the book and the results were less than stellar. His memoir stands mostly as a defense of his career, but can be a frustrating read as it leaves out significant details and is obviously slanted in areas.

In 1962, MacArthur gave his last major speech, appropriately at West Point. His alma mater was honoring him with the Sylvanus Thayer award for outstanding service to his country. He probably should not have gone. MacArthur was in terrible health, suffering from biliary cirrhosis—the effects of gallstones that were pressing on his bile duct. Jean begged him not to go, but he ignored her pleas. "I will attend the Thayer Award ceremony," he said, "if I have to crawl there on my hands and knees."[7]

MacArthur wanted to make a good impression and prepared for the occasion by memorizing his two-thousand-word speech as he paced throughout his apartment while wearing a robe and puffing on his corncob pipe.[8] When the day arrived MacArthur was barely over the flu and looked every bit of his eighty-two years. Yet, as with all of the challenges he faced throughout his life, MacArthur faced them head-on and almost always came out on top. This night would be no different. Reminiscent of the actors and actresses he was enthralled with on Broadway stages, on May 12, 1962, MacArthur gave a stellar performance. For an hour he captivated the wide-eyed cadets with passages from former speeches, which seemed fresh to their young ears. Even though at times his voiced cracked, there was still gusto in his delivery. As an orator few could rival him. And in typical MacArthur style, he ended the speech on a dramatic note:

> I listen vainly, but with thirsty ear, for the witching melody of faint bugles blowing reveille, of far drums beating the long roll. In my dreams I hear again the crash of guns, the rattle of musketry, and the mournful mutter of the battlefield. But in the evening of my life, I always come back to West Point. Always there echoes and re-echoes in my ears—Duty, Honor, Country. Today marks my final roll call with you. But I want you to know that when I cross the river my last conscious thought will be of the Corps . . . and the Corps . . . and the Corps. I bid you farewell.[9]

Declining health marked the two years following this rousing speech. His doctors wanted to operate, but MacArthur refused to allow them. It took the convincing of the U.S. Army Surgeon General and the offer of Air Force One by President Lyndon Johnson to take him from New York to Washington, before MacArthur agreed to have the surgery. On March 1, 1964, he checked into Walter Reed and during the course of two weeks he had two operations. Just when it appeared he was recovering, his doctors said a third surgery was necessary, but MacArthur was too weak and he lapsed into a coma that he never came out of. MacArthur died on April 5, 1964. At his bedside were his wife, his son, and his good friend Courtney Whitney.

Newspaper headlines around the world splashed "Nation Mourns A Hero." Forty-six years after he led the capture of the Cote de Châttillon, twenty years after he triumphantly returned the American forces to the Philippines, and thirteen years after he created the masterful Inchon Landing, Douglas MacArthur, America's General, was dead.

As one would expect, MacArthur's funeral was truly astonishing. At the urging of President Kennedy, whose untimely death occurred the year before, MacArthur had planned the event. First, there was the six-cannon salute at West Point in front of twenty-five hundred cadets standing at attention. Then thirty-five thousand watched as his casket proceeded down Manhattan's major thoroughfares. Millions more witnessed this on television. Then his body was taken to Washington to rest in state at the Capitol where a solemn President Johnson placed a wreath of red, white, and blue flowers at the foot of MacArthur's coffin. The general's remains were flown to Norfolk, Virginia, for burial. He had chosen Norfolk because it was his mother's birthplace and was willing to accommodate him with a memorial and archive. A service took place at Saint Paul's Episcopal Church, Norfolk, and then the old soldier was laid to rest.

Legacy

DOUGLAS MACARTHUR'S LEGACY as an American icon was sealed on May 12, 1962. His address that day to the West Point Corps of Cadets was spellbinding. After receiving the Sylvanus Thayer award from superintendant General William Westmoreland, MacArthur commenced his speech on a humorous note: "As I was leaving the hotel this morning, the doorman asked me, 'Where are you bound for, General?' And when I replied West Point, he remarked, 'beautiful place, have you ever been there before?' "[1]

Among the more than twenty-one hundred at Washington Hall that afternoon was Cadet Larry Bennett. He listened intently as the eighty-two-year-old general's words evoked the true meaning of what it was like to serve one's country. His voice was at times strong and at other moments weak, but he got the point across. "Your mission," he told them, "remains fixed, determined, inviolable—it is to win our wars."

Bennett recalled that when MacArthur looked into the crowd assembled before him, which he did for the entire thirty-minute speech since he spoke from memory, it was as though he was "talking only to me."[2] It is likely that all the cadets felt that way. MacArthur had the ability to draw in his audience, whether he was talking to one person or to thousands. With the cadets on the edge of their seats, MacArthur drew his talk to a close. MacArthur then saluted Jean, who was sitting on the poop deck. Cadet Bennett said there was stunned silence. The audience had just witnessed history and wanted to savor that moment for as long as possible.

When pondering the greater meaning of MacArthur's speech, historian Rick Atkinson wrote: "In the coming months they would hear the speech again and again. In their classes, in their barracks, in their sleep, they would hear the general's call to arms." The average citizen could hear the speech as well. One of the cadets smartly brought in a reel-to-reel tape and recorded the speech for posterity. Later it was made available for purchase as a 33 rpm recording.

To fully understand MacArthur one must look back to his formative years, heavily influenced by a strong-willed grandfather and nurturing parents. Judge MacArthur taught Douglas's father that to succeed in the world it is important to display traits of versatility and nobility. Arthur then passed these words of wisdom on to Douglas. As army commanders, father and son both excelled as combat leaders. As administrators, they demonstrated professional excellence, fierce ambition, and superior intelligence. Arthur MacArthur led his country with dignity and abstained from typical soldier's vices such as excessive cussing, drinking, gambling, and promiscuity. Douglas maintained his life the same way. He also learned the MacArthur attribute of loyalty and stuck by members of his staff, never publicly second-guessing their actions. They in turn remained loyal to him and stood by his side during some of the most challenging moments in history. MacArthur's mother taught him about courage, to stand up for what he believed in, and to hold his head up high.

There is no better place to ponder the legacy of Douglas MacArthur than at the MacArthur Memorial in Norfolk, Virginia. Encompassing an entire city block, the more than seventy-five thousand visitors who pay homage each year first see a larger-than-life statue of the general. Inside the museum there are memorabilia gathered from a lifetime of service: his corncob pipe, sunglasses, uniforms, weapons, and other precious mementoes in display cases. In the rotunda are two beautiful tombs that hold the remains of Douglas and Jean. Another building houses MacArthur's personal papers and his enormous book collection, which equates to the grandeur of a presidential library. Such an impressive memorial seems appropriate as MacArthur is better known to some people than many of the commanders in chief who have led the nation.

Today Douglas MacArthur is mostly unknown to the younger generation, but this is certainly not true for current and future West Point cadets, who are indoctrinated with the campaigns and speeches of the great general. Yet anyone, young or old, wanting to appreciate the United States' involvement in the twentieth century and how that continues to change in the current century would benefit from learning about MacArthur and the world in which he served his country. Through his leadership and conviction on the battlefield, America persevered during times of war.

Although MacArthur's legacy is associated with his military commands, there is little reason to doubt that had he been elected to lead the United States from the White House, his resilience and knowledge of world affairs would have also made the nation strong during peacetime. Even though MacArthur never got the chance to serve at the highest level, he will always remain as someone, no matter how glorious or controversial, who could be counted upon to give his best and do what he thought was correct.

"Old soldiers never die, they just fade away." And like the old soldier of that ballad, I now close my military career and just fade away—an old soldier who tried to do his duty as God gave him the light to see that duty. Goodbye.

Notes

CHAPTER ONE

1. Kenneth Ray Young, *The General's General: The Life and Times of Arthur MacArthur* (Boulder: Westview), 3–4.

2. Ibid., 10–13.

3. Ibid., 79.

4. D. Clayton James, *The Years of MacArthur, Volume I, 1880–1941* (Boston: Houghton, Mifflin Company, 1970), 21.

5. William Manchester, *American Caesar: Douglas MacArthur, 1880–1964* (Boston: Little, Brown and Company, 1978), 42.

6. Ibid., 23.

7. Young, 132.

8. Ibid., 120–34.

CHAPTER TWO

1. Young, 137–38.

2. Ibid., 141–44.

3. Ibid., 147.

4. Douglas MacArthur, *Reminiscences* (New York: McGraw Hill Book Company, 1964)., 5.

5. Geoffrey Perrett, *Old Soldiers Never Die: The Life of Douglas MacArthur* (New York: Random House, 1996), 21.

6. James, 62.

7. Ibid., 65.

8. Ibid., 66.

9. Manchester, 47.

10. MacArthur, 25.

11. Ibid., 48.

12. Rick Atkinson, *The Long Gray Line: The American Journey of West Point's Class of 1966* (New York: Holt Paperbacks: 2009), 15–16.

13. James, 69–70.

14. Manchester, 50–51.

15. MacArthur, 25–26.

16. Ibid., 27.

CHAPTER THREE

1. MacArthur, 26.

2. James, 43.

3. Ibid., 39.

4. Ibid., 40.

5. Ibid., 96.

6. MacArthur, 35.

7. Young, 340.

8. MacArthur, 36.

CHAPTER FOUR

1. MacArthur, 40.

2. James, 126.

3. MacArthur, 43–44.

4. Perret, 74.

CHAPTER FIVE

1. James, 142.

2. Ibid., 143.

3. Ibid., 148.

4. The puttee was a legging worn by American and British soldiers. Beau Brummel was considered a fashion trendsetter in England during the early part of the nineteenth century and his name is associated with men who are fashion conscious.

5. James, 169–71.

6. Ibid., 189.

7. Manchester, 97.

8. MacArthur, 58.

9. MacArthur actually received in 1918 a three-sixteenth-inch "silver

citation star" for gallantry in action. In accordance with War Department regulations, the small star was affixed to the ribbon of the relevant campaign medal. In MacArthur's case, the citation star was pinned onto the ribbon of his World War I Victory medal. The full-sized Silver Star medal was not actually established until 1932, when MacArthur was chief of staff. It was made retroactive to World War I, which meant a recipient like MacArthur could then request a Silver Star Medal in lieu of the earlier ribbon device.

      10. Kevin Hymel, http://www.armyhistory.org/ahf2.aspx?pgID=877&id=105&exCompID=56.

CHAPTER SIX

      1. MacArthur, 70.

      2. Ibid., 66.

      3. Ibid., 67.

      4. Ibid., 70.

      5. Ibid., 72.

CHAPTER SEVEN

      1. James, 26.

      2. Ibid., 268.

      3. Langford, Gary D., Capt., 1919: *MacArthur's Vision of West Point's Future Warriors* (USMA Digital Library, December 5, 1991). [[need page number]]

      4. Ibid., 66.

      5. MacArthur, 81.

      6. Langford, 18.

      7. James, 259.

      8. Ibid., 291.

      9. Donald Smythe, *Pershing: General of the Armies* (Bloomington: University of Indiana Press, 1986), 276–77.

      10. James, 290.

      11. Perret, 15–127.

CHAPTER EIGHT

      1. MacArthur, 85.

      2. Many thanks to historian Douglas Waller, author of *A Question of Loyalty*, for his insight into the Mitchell trial.

      3. James, 317–18.

      4. Ibid.

      5. Ibid., 323.

6. MacArthur, 83.

7. James, 328.

8. Ibid., 332.

9. Ibid.

10. Ibid.

11. Ibid.

12. Ibid., 341.

13. MacArthur, 89.

CHAPTER NINE

1. MacArthur, 90.

2. James, 376–77.

3. Carlo D'Este, *Dwight D. Eisenhower: A Soldier's Life, 1890–1945* (New York: Henry Holt, 2002), 220.

4. Ibid.

5. Ibid., 221.

6. Ibid., 222.

7. Ibid.

8. Ibid., 223.

9. MacArthur, 95.

10. Ibid., 95–96.

11. Carol D'Este, "Dwight D. Eisenhower: MacArthur's Aide," *MHQ: Quarterly Journal of Military History*, Winter 2003, 218–21.

CHAPTER TEN

1. D'Este, "Dwight D. Eisenhower: MacArthur's Aide," 101.

2. Ibid.

3. MacArthur, 101.

4. James, 446.

5. MacArthur, 102.

6. D'Este, "Dwight D. Eisenhower: MacArthur's Aide," 226.

7. Dwight D. Eisenhower, *At Ease: Stories I Tell to Friends* (Garden City, New York: Doubleday & Company, Inc., 1967), 214.

8. Manchester, 165.

9. Ibid.

10. Eisenhower, 224.

11. Ibid., 225.

12. Perret, 188.

13. D'Este, "Dwight D. Eisenhower: MacArthur's Aide," 238.

CHAPTER ELEVEN

1. James, 513.

2. MacArthur, 106–7.

3. James, 537.

4. Eisenhower, 226.

5. MacArthur, 107.

6. James, 525.

7. Eisenhower, 231.

8. Ibid.

9. Ibid.

CHAPTER TWELVE

1. D. Clayton James, *The Years of MacArthur, Volume II, 1941–1945* (Boston: Houghton Mifflin Company, 1975), 78

2. James, *Volume I*, 584.

3. Manchester, 205.

4. Many thanks to Air Force historian Roger Miller for his comments on Brereton and the events of December 8, 1941.

5. Louis Morton, *The Fall of the Philippines* (Washington, D.C.: Washington Center for Military History, 1953), 88.

6. Ibid.

7. MacArthur, 120.

8. Ibid., 121.

CHAPTER THIRTEEN

1. MacArthur, 131.

2. Ibid., 132.

3. Perret, 280.

4. MacArthur, 145.

5. James, *Volume II*, 146–47.

6. Ibid., 147.

7. Ibid., 150

CHAPTER FOURTEEN

1. James, *Volume II*, 110.

2. Ronald Spector, *Eagle Against the Sun: The American War with Japan* (New York: Free Press, 1985), 144.

3. MacArthur, 165.

4. James, *Volume II*, 385–86.

5. Charles A. Willoughby, *Reports of General MacArthur: Japanese Operations in the Southwest Pacific Area, Volume II, Part I* (Washington, D.C.: CMH, 1994), 100.

CHAPTER FIFTEEN

1. Manchester, 364.
2. Ibid., 365.
3. Ibid., 366.
4. Ibid., 378-79.
5. MacArthur, 216-17.
6. James, *Volume II*, 622.
7. Spector, 542.

CHAPTER SIXTEEN

1. James, *Volume II*, 790.
2. MacArthur, 275.
3. Ibid., 271-72.
4. D. Clayton James, *The Years of MacArthur: Triumph and Disaster, Volume III, 1946-1964* (Boston: Houghton Mifflin Company, 1985), 373.
5. Ibid., 373-74.
6. James, *Volume II*, 663-64.

CHAPTER SEVENTEEN

1. MacArthur, 327.
2. James interview with Edwin Simmons, Douglas MacArthur Memorial Archives and Library, Norfolk, VA.
3. James, *Volume III*, 597-98.
4. Ibid., 598.
5. Ibid., 603.

EPILOGUE

1. MacArthur, 400-5.
2. James, *Volume III*, 635.
3. Perret, 577.
4. Manchester, 701.
5. Perret, 578-79.
6. Ibid., 579.
7. Ibid., 584.
8. Atkinson, 31.
9. James, *Volume III*, 678-80.

LEGACY

1. MacArthur, 423.
2. Many thanks to Larry Bennett for his recollections about the Duty, Honor, Country speech.

Bibliography

Atkinson, Rick. *The Long Gray Line: The American Journey of West Point's Class of 1966.* New York: Holt Paperbacks, 2009.

Bartsch, William H. *December 8, 1941: MacArthur's Pearl Harbor.* Texas A&M University Press, 2003.

D'Este, Carlo. "Dwight D. Eisenhower: A Soldier's Life, 1890-1945. New York: Henry Holt, 2002.

D'Este, Carlo. "Dwight D. Eisenhower: MacArthur's Aide in the 1930s." *MHQ: The Quarterly Journal of Military History,* winter 2003.

Eisenhower, Dwight D., *At Ease: Stories I Tell to Friends.* Garden City, New York: Doubleday & Company, Inc., 1967.

Ferrell, Robert H. *The Question of MacArthur's Reputation: Cote De Chatillon, October 14–16, 1918.* Columbia: University of Missouri Press, 2008.

Ganoe, William Addleman. *MacArthur Up Close.* Vantage Press, 1962.

Hunt, Frazier. *The Untold Story of Douglas MacArthur.* Devin Adair, 1954.

James, D. Clayton. *The Years of MacArthur, three volumes.* Boston: Houghton Mifflin Company, 1970-1985.

Langford, Gary D., Capt. *1919: MacArthur's Vision of West Point's Future Warriors.* USMA Digital Library, December 5, 1991.

Leary, William A. *MacArthur and the American Century: A Reader.* Nebraska, 2001.

MacArthur, Douglas. *Reminiscences*. New York: McGraw Hill Book Company, 1964.

Manchester, William. *American Caesar: Douglas MacArthur, 1880–1964*. Boston: Little, Brown and Company, 1978.

Morton, Louis. *The Fall of the Philippines*. Washington: Center for Military History, 1953.

Perret, Geoffrey. *Old Soldiers Never Die: The Life of Douglas MacArthur*. New York: Random House, 1996.

Reilly, Henry J. *Americans All: The Rainbow at War*. Columbus: The F. J. Heer Publishers, 1936.

Smythe, Donald. *Pershing: General of the Armies*. Bloomington: University of Indiana Press, 1986.

Spector, Ronald. *Eagle Against the Sun: The American War with Japan* (New York: Free Press, 1985).

Waller, Douglas C. *A Question of Loyalty : Gen. Billy Mitchell and the Court-Martial That Gripped the Nation*. New York: Harper Collins, 2004.

Willoughby, Charles A. *Reports of General MacArthur: Japanese Operations in the Southwest Pacific Area, Volume II, Part I*. Washington: CMH, 1994.

Young, Kenneth Ray. *The General's General: The Life and Times of Arthur MacArthur*. Boulder: Westview Press, 1994.

Acknowledgments

THROUGHOUT THE PROCESS of writing this book there are many people who had a hand in bringing it to fruition. I am grateful to the editors and staff of my publisher, Thomas Nelson, the staff of the MacArthur Memorial Archives and Library, the faculty at the United States Naval Academy and my colleagues and friends at the National Archives and Records Administration. Of course I would like to thank my family and close friends for their encouragement. Despite the generous assistance I received while researching and writing the book, any errors are my responsibility alone.

About the Author

MITCHELL YOCKELSON IS an Investigative Archivist at the National Archives and Records Administration and an instructor of history at the United States Naval Academy and Norwich University. He received his undergraduate degree from Frostburg State University, a Masters degree from George Mason University and a Doctorate from the Royal Military College of Science, Cranfield University. He has authored numerous articles and book reviews on various aspects of military history and is a frequent media consultant. His first book, *Borrowed Soldiers: American Under British Command, 1918*, was published in 2008.